KU-020-492

COUNTRY

Kitchen
Cutouts

COUNTRY
Kitchen
Cutouts

Lee Lindeman
& Pat Harste

 Sterling Publishing Co., Inc. New York

The authors would like to thank George Ross for the beautiful color photography and Stephen Donelian for the impeccable black-and-white pictures. A special thanks to Eleanor Levie for the use of her lovely home and to Christine Noonan for her invaluable assistance. We are also grateful to Dove Brushes, Plaid Enterprises, for supplying the Folk Art Acrylic Color, and to WesTrim Crafts for supplying the beads.

Library of Congress Cataloging-in-Publication Data

Lindeman, Lee.
    Country kitchen cutouts / Lee Lindeman & Pat Harste.
       p.   cm.
    Includes index.
    ISBN 0-8069-0370-8
    1. Woodwork.   2. House furnishings.   I. Harste, Pat.   II. Title.
TT180.L564   1994
684'.08—dc20   93-43891
                                                    CIP

10 9 8 7 6 5 4 3 2 1

Published by Sterling Publishing Company, Inc.
387 Park Avenue South, New York, N.Y. 10016
© 1994 by Lee Lindeman and Pat Harste
Distributed in Canada by Sterling Publishing
% Canadian Manda Group, P.O. Box 920, Station U
Toronto, Ontario, Canada M8Z 5P9
Distributed in Great Britain and Europe by Cassell PLC
Villiers House, 41/47 Strand, London WC2N 5JE, England
Distributed in Australia by Capricorn Link (Australia) Pty Ltd.
P.O. Box 6651, Baulkham Hills, Business Centre, NSW 2153, Australia
Manufactured in the United States of America
All rights reserved

Sterling ISBN 0-8069-0370-8

Contents

• • • • • • • • • • • •

[Color photos follow page 32]

Introduction

• • • • • • • • • • • •

Before You Begin

To save time, read through the project's directions to both familiarize yourself with them and enable you to gather the materials, tools, and equipment you will need. Refer to the General Directions section for the various techniques used in making the projects.

Materials

The Materials list at the beginning of each project is always presented in the same order, making it an easy reference when gathering or shopping for materials. Lumber, dowelling, miscellaneous wood items (such as beads and axle pegs), drill bits, brads, and screws are listed from the smallest size of the product to the largest. The paint colors are listed in the order in which they are used. The last item listed is the type of protective coating to be applied. Unless otherwise specified, use a water-base varnish in the type of finish recommended.

Lumber and dowelling estimates allow for waste as well as a safety margin when handling them in a scroll saw. The dimension of the lumber specified in the Materials list is the nominal or premilled size. For example, $\frac{1}{4} \times 5\frac{1}{4}$ clear pine lattice actually measures $\frac{7}{32} \times 5\frac{3}{16}''$.

The sizes listed for an axle peg in a Materials list are the diameter and length of the shank, excluding the cap. The size of the drill bit used to drill the axle-peg hole matches the diameter of the axle peg. The amount of shank that will extend from the axle-peg hole after assembly is noted in the project's directions. There are no industry standards for axle pegs, so minor adjustments may be necessary if the exact size of the axle peg listed is unavailable. Use a drill bit that matches the diameter of the axle peg. Drill a test hole in scrap wood. The axle peg should fit tightly into the hole. Adjust the peg-hole depth by drilling slightly deeper or shallower to accommodate a slightly longer or shorter shank. An axle peg that is too long can be shortened with a coping saw.

Tools and Equipment

The following is a list of the tools and equipment required for the projects. Some of the items are not required for every project, and any additional tools needed are listed in the project's Materials list.

Pencil   for tracing patterns and marking measurements

Tracing paper   for tracing or enlarging patterns

Graphite paper   for transferring patterns onto wood

Dressmaker's carbon paper   for transferring patterns onto fabric

Masking tape   for securing patterns while they are being transferred

Cellophane tape   for taping multiple-part patterns together

Double-sided masking tape   for adhering stacked-wood pieces together before sawing

Sharp scissors   for cutting out fabric pieces and trims

Wire cutters   for cutting lengths of wire

18″ metal ruler   for measuring and as a guide when drawing straight lines

Safety glasses   for eye protection

Scroll saw   for cutting wood and long lengths of dowelling

Coping saw   for cutting short lengths of dowelling or axle-peg shanks

Whittling knife   for rounding edges, making angles, and cutting beads in half

Wood vise   for holding a piece securely when using a coping saw or drilling into the edge of a piece

Clamps   for clamping wood pieces being bonded or glued, or securing wood pieces to the work surface when drilling into the face of a piece. (Use spring clamps, C-clamps, bar clamps, or handscrews.)

Hand drill   for drilling holes (An adjustable-speed power drill can also be used.)

Drill bits and spade bits   See the project's Materials list for sizes.

Drill stop   for drilling accurate hole depths

½″ countersink bit   for drilling a cone-shaped depression into a drilled pilot hole so that the head of an inserted and tightened screw will be below the surface of the wood

Ice pick   for making pilot holes for screw eyes

Small hammer   for driving brads and cutting beads in half

Nail set   for sinking brads below the surface of the wood and making an indention in the wood before using a hand drill

Screwdrivers   for driving screws (Use a screwdriver that matches the screw-head type.)

Medium (150-grit), fine (220-grit), and super-fine (400-grit) sandpapers   for sanding edges and surfaces smooth, and sanding between coats of paint or finish

Tack cloth   for wiping sawdust from wood pieces after they have been sanded (Store the tack cloth in a screw-top jar to prevent it from drying out.)

Wood glue   for adhering raw wood to raw wood (For applications where clamping is not possible, we recommend using a cyanoacrylate wood glue, which bonds in seconds.)

Waterproof wood glue   for projects that may need to be washed after use

Tacky glue (extra-thick white glue)   Use, as specified in the directions, for adhering fabric, trims, and painted wood to painted wood.

Small dish   for holding glue

Toothpicks   for applying glue to small areas

½″ flat brush   for applying glue to large areas

Paste wood filler   for filling bead half-holes and gaps in construction and covering countersunk screws and brads

No. 000, 5, and 7 round brushes   for painting details

¼″, ½″, and 1″ flat brushes   for painting small to large areas

½ × ½″, 1 × 1″, and 2 × 2″ cubes of cellulose sponge   for sponge painting

Paper towels   for sponge painting and drying brushes

Paint palette or ceramic dish   for holding paint

Jar and water   for washing brushes

Craft knife   for cutting decorative adhesive coverings

Safety Precautions

- Always wear safety glasses when sawing, drilling, whittling, or sanding.
- Always wear short sleeves and keep long hair tied back and out of the way when using power tools.
- Never wear rings, bracelets, or a watch when using power tools.
- To prevent interruptions when using power tools, it is best to take the phone off the hook and make sure that small children and pets are safely out of the way.
- When using a scroll saw, make sure that the safety guard is down or in position before you begin to saw.
- Always turn a scroll saw off when it is not being used.
- Never turn off a scroll saw while the blade is still in the wood as the blade could break when power is restored.

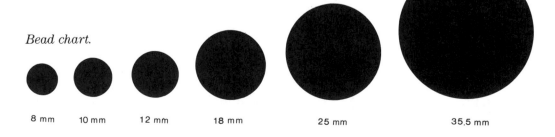

Bead chart.

8 mm   10 mm   12 mm   18 mm   25 mm   35.5 mm

General Directions

• • • • • • • • • • • •

Making the Patterns

Most of the patterns in this book are actual size and ready to use. Secure tracing paper over the pattern, and use a pencil to trace the outline as well as painting lines, dashed positioning lines, stars or dots for pilot holes, and so on.

To enlarge a reduced pattern, you can either have the pattern enlarged at a photocopying shop (each box of the grid equals 1″) or enlarge it by hand.

To enlarge a pattern by hand, first draw lines across the pattern to connect the grid lines. Count the boxes across each edge to determine the size of tracing paper you will need. Rule the tracing paper into 1″ squares, making the same number of squares that are on the pattern. Then copy the pattern, line for line, onto the tracing paper.

To complete a half-pattern, trace the half-pattern shown in the book onto tracing paper. Turn the tracing over, align the dashed line on the tracing over the dashed line on the pattern in the book, and trace the half-pattern again.

To complete a multiple-part pattern, trace each part of the pattern onto separate sheets of tracing paper. Assemble the pattern by aligning the dotted line on one part over the dotted line on an adjacent part, and tape the parts together. Repeat until the pattern is completed.

Left and Right

Unless otherwise stated, left and right always refer to an animal's left and right sides. The left and right of all other items indicate your left and right as you view the item on the work surface.

Transferring Patterns and Marks

For maximum strength, position the patterns on the wood so that the longest dimension of the pattern is parallel with the grain of the wood.

To transfer a pattern onto wood, place graphite paper over the wood with the graphite side facing down. Use masking tape to secure it to the wood. Place the pattern on top and secure it with tape. Use a pencil to retrace all lines and dots or stars onto the wood; then remove the pattern and graphite paper.

Cut out the piece, using a scroll saw. If a project has two identical sides, turn the pattern over to reverse the image and transfer all lines and dots to the other side of the piece. Some projects (such as the Horse Weather Vane) don't have the same leg positions on both sides of the body, so be sure to read the project's directions before proceeding.

To transfer a pattern onto fabric, tape the fabric to the work surface. Place dressmaker's carbon paper (carbon side down) over the fabric and tape to secure. Place the pattern on top and tape it also. Use a pencil to retrace all lines.

Stacking Wood

For fast cutting of two identical pieces, use double-sided tape to adhere two lengths of lumber together. Be sure that the grain of both lengths runs in the same direction. Transfer the pattern outline to the top of the stacked wood, and cut the pieces out using a scroll saw. If the pieces must also be drilled for pilot holes, mark the hole positions and drill through the stack before separating the pieces.

Bonding Wood

To bond two pieces of wood together, run a continuous, thin bead of wood glue evenly across the surface of each piece (see 1). Place the glued faces together with the edges aligned and clamp at each corner. Allow the bonded wood to set for at least four hours before transferring the pattern onto it and cutting it out.

Cutting Wood

If more than one pattern outline has been transferred onto a length of wood, cut between the outlines to make separate, more manageable pieces.

To cut the shank of an axle peg or short lengths of dowelling, place the item in a wood vise and make the cut with a coping saw.

Whittling

Round off edges with a whittling knife (see 2). Always work away from yourself and use firm, short strokes. Use the whittling knife to shave off edges and add contours to animals, trees, bushes, and so on. Use the color section and the photographs at the beginning of the projects as guides to contouring. Finish the contouring by sanding.

Angles are specified to be whittled on the underside of a piece so that the piece will angle out from the assembly and add dimension to the project. Whittle from the dashed line on the pattern towards the dot to create an angle with a specified thickness at the dot. Sand the angle surface flat as described in the following section.

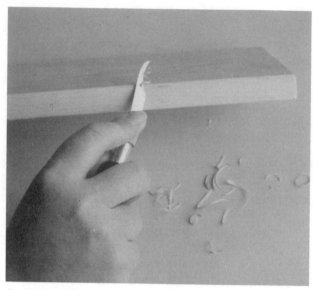

2. Rounding off an edge with a whittling knife.

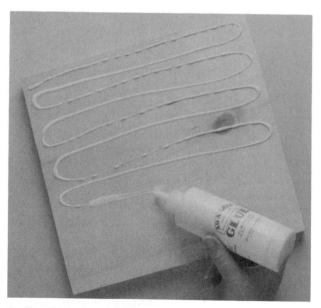

3. Using a nail set to make an indentation in the wood before using a hand drill.

1. Running a continuous, thin bead of wood glue across the face of each piece is the first step in bonding wood.

Sanding

Thoroughly sand all pieces before assembling. Use medium, then fine-grit, sandpaper, and wipe with a tack cloth.

For edges, you can either sand by hand or use the sanding capabilities of your scroll saw. For large areas, use a sanding block or a power palm sander. It's safest to sand small pieces by hand. When sanding whittled angles to make a flat surface for gluing, the easiest method to use is to rub the angle on a piece of sandpaper that has been adhered to a piece of scrap wood or the work surface.

Drilling Holes

For accurate drilling into the edge of a piece, secure the piece in a wood vise so that the marked position of the hole to be drilled is facing up and centered on the width of the vise.

If a hand drill is to be used, make a small indentation at the mark with a hammer and nail set. This will help the drill bit to bite into the wood when you start drilling (see 3). This step isn't necessary if a power drill is used.

Hold the drill perpendicular to the surface to be drilled. Drill the hole to the depth specified in the directions. For accurate hole depths, use a drill stop (see 4).

When drilling into the face of a piece, place the piece on top of scrap lumber and secure both to the work surface with a clamp. To avoid scarring the wood, insert a scrap of $\frac{1}{4} \times 5\frac{1}{4}$ lattice between the clamp and the piece. Drilling through the piece and into the scrap lumber ensures a smooth hole edge on the underside of the piece (see 5).

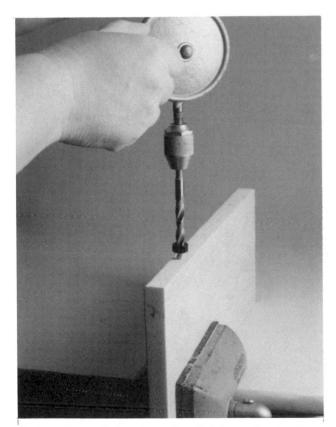

4. Drilling a hole with a hand drill and a drill stop.

5. Drilling through two identical pieces and into scrap lumber.

Gluing and Clamping

Use wood glue whenever you adhere raw wood to raw wood. We recommend that a quick-setting wood glue (such as a cyanoacrylate wood glue) be used when the construction makes it impossible to clamp the pieces together. When using a quick-setting wood glue, the pieces can be held firmly together by hand for the few seconds it takes for a permanent bond to form.

Regular wood glue can be used for adhering axle pegs or applications where clamping is possible. Use spring clamps, C-clamps, bar clamps, or handscrews. Clamping isn't needed when screws or brads are used in addition to glue. Use a waterproof wood glue (as specified) for those projects that may need to be washed after use.

Tacky glue, an extra-thick white glue, is used when adhering fabrics and trims to a painted surface or in the rare instances when painted wood is adhered to painted wood.

Countersinking Screws

Projects requiring screws in their assembly have a more finished appearance if time is taken to countersink the screws. After drilling a pilot hole, fit the drill with a countersink bit. Use this bit to drill a cone-shaped hole into the pilot hole to allow the screw head, when fully tightened, to sink about ⅛″ below the surface of the wood. After inserting the screw, fill the hole with paste wood filler, allow to dry, and sand smooth.

Countersinking Brads

Brads should also be countersunk. After driving the brad almost flat to the wood's surface, place a nail set on its head and hammer until the head is ⅟₁₆″ below the surface of the wood. Fill the depression with paste wood filler, allow to dry, and sand smooth.

Cutting Beads in Half

To cut a bead in half, place the bead on the work surface with the hole facing up. Place the middle of the whittling knife's blade over the middle of the hole, and firmly tap the middle top of the blade with a hammer. Sand the cut surface of each bead half smooth by rubbing it on fine-grit sandpaper (see 6).

Painting

When painting, don't allow the paint to flow into holes drilled in the project, unless the directions instruct otherwise. For the best coverage, apply at least two coats of each color of paint. Allow each color to dry thoroughly between coats or before proceeding to the next step in the directions. For the best paint adhesion, sand lightly between the coats with super-fine-grit sandpaper and wipe with a tack cloth.

Sponge Painting

Moisten the sponge with water and squeeze it almost dry. Dab the sponge into the paint and tamp it onto paper towels to remove the excess. Then dab the sponge onto the project, making an irregular pattern by changing the angle of the sponge's surface with each dabbing.

Finishing

When painting and/or assembly is completed, and before adhering trims, apply a protective coating. Unless otherwise specified in the Materials List, use a water-base varnish in the type of finish recommended. Apply two or more coats, using super-fine-grit sandpaper to sand lightly between the coats, and then wipe with a tack cloth.

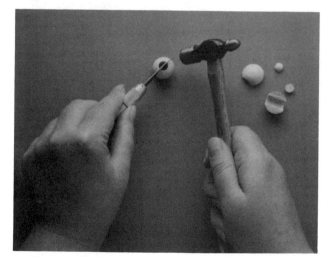

6. Using a hammer and whittling knife to cut a bead in half.

PROJECTS

1. Schoolhouse Desk Lamp

- 28″ length of ¼ × 5¼ clear pine lattice
- 13″ length of ½ × 5½ clear pine lattice
- 2″ length of 1 × 1 clear pine
- 6½ × 85⁄8 × ¾″ pine plaque, with a roman-ogee routed edge (or an 85⁄8″ length of 1 × 8 clear pine)
- One 18-mm, small-hole, unfinished, round wood bead
- Four ½″-diameter, oval-top, screw hole plugs
- Fifteen ice-cream sticks
- Drill bits: No. 61 (wire gauge), 1⁄16″, 5⁄64″ (Note: Use a bit that matches the diameter of the flagpole), and 3⁄8″
- Two #6 × ¾″ flat-head wood screws
- Sixteen #19 × ½″ wire brads
- Twenty-four #18 × ¾″ wire brads
- Router fitted with a roman-ogee bit that has a ¼″ cutting radius (Note: This is not needed if a prerouted plaque is used.)
- One 9-mm, gold, flat nail-head stud
- ½″-high, vinyl, self-adhesive letters
- Orange and brown curly chenille hair
- 12″ length of threaded lamp pipe (Note: If necessary, use a hacksaw to cut the pipe to the specified length.)
- One lock nut to fit the lamp pipe
- One lamp socket (Note: The base of the socket must be threaded inside to accept the lamp pipe.)
- 6′ length of lamp wire
- One electrical plug
- One 1¼ × 13⁄10″ paper flag on a 5⁄64″-diameter × 2½″-long flagpole
- 12 × 12 × 8″ rectangular lamp shade, fitted with a bulb clip
- Acrylic paints: red, light grey, dark grey, black, ecru, medium-green, medium-blue-grey, brown, dark green, light pink, and dark pink
- High-gloss finish

Schoolhouse Desk Lamp. Top: *front and right view;* bottom: *back and left view.*

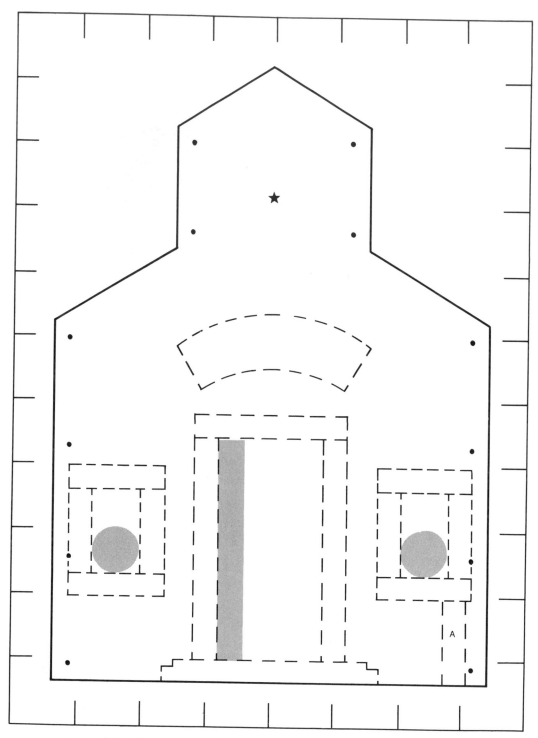

1–1. Schoolhouse, front. Each square equals 1". Enlarge and cut one.

Schoolhouse Desk Lamp*

1. Use the prerouted plaque for the base, or trim the width of the 8⅝" length of 1 × 8 pine to 6½". Rout the edge, using the roman-ogee bit.

2. Cut one front (1–1) and one back (1–2) from ¼" plywood.

3. Cut one lower-left side (1–3) and one lower-right side (1–4) from ½ × 5½ pine lattice.

4. Transfer the outlines of the tinted (gluing) areas onto the fronts of 1–1, 1–2, 1–3, and 1–4.

5. Cut one banner (1–5) and one tree (1–6) from ¼ × 5¼ pine lattice. Transfer the dashed line on 1–6 onto the back of the left side of the tree.

6. Cut two small shrubs (1–7) and two large shrubs (1–8) from ¼ × 5¼ pine lattice. Mark one small shrub A and the other small shrub B. Mark one large shrub C and the other large shrub D. (These letters correspond to the letters on 1–1, 1–3, and 1–4.) Transfer the light dashed line on 1–7 onto the back of shrub A and the heavy dashed line onto the back of shrub B. Transfer the outline of the tinted (gluing) area on 1–8 onto the front of shrub C and the dashed line on 1–8 onto the back of shrub C. (There is no additional marking for shrub D.)

7. Cut one bottom step (1–9) and one door (1–10) from ¼ × 5¼ pine lattice.

8. Cut one chimney (1–11) from 1 × 1 clear pine.

9. Cut two 2 × 4¼" rectangles from ½ × 5½ lattice for the upper-left and upper-right sides.

10. Cut four 2⅝ × 5¾" rectangles from ¼ × 5¼ lattice for the roof pieces. Tilt the scroll-saw table to 35 degrees, and trim one long end of each piece to a 55-degree bevel.

11. Draw two lines ⅞" from and parallel with the short edges of each roof piece. On the two lower-roof pieces, make two marks on each line ½" from each long edge. On the two upper-roof pieces, measure from the angled edge (the roof peak) and on each line mark ½" and 1⅜".

12. Using the No. 61 bit, drill pilot holes though the roof pieces at the marks.

---

*Refer to the General Directions for the techniques needed to complete this project.

13. Using the No. 61 bit, drill pilot holes through the front (1–1) and back (1–2), where indicated by the dots on the patterns.

14. Using the No. 61 bit, drill pilot holes through the tree (1–6) and door (1–10), where indicated by the stars on the patterns.

15. Using the 5/64" bit, drill a ½"-deep flagpole hole in the front (1–1), where indicated by the star on the pattern. (See the note in the Materials List.) Drill at a 75-degree angle, aiming the bit towards the bottom back of the piece.

16. Draw two lines 1 3/16" from and parallel with the short edges of the base. Locate the middle of each line, and, using the 1/16" bit, drill pilot holes through the base at each mark.

17. Locate the middle of the base. Using the ⅜" bit, drill a hole through the base for the lamp pipe.

18. To create the angle on the back of the door (1–10), whittle a flat area, from the dashed line towards the edge marked with the dots, so that the thickness at the edge is 3/32".

19. Glue the front and back (1–1 and 1–2) to the edges of the lower-left (1–3) and lower-right (1–4) sides. Secure with sixteen #18 × ¾" brads nailed through the pilot holes in the front and back.

20. Glue the upper-left and upper-right sides between the front (1–1) and back (1–2), aligning their top and bottom edges with the angle cuts in the front and back. Secure with eight #18 × ¾" brads nailed through the pilot holes in the front and back.

21. Apply glue to the bottom edge of the assembly. Center the assembly over the base, and secure it with two screws driven through the pilot holes in the base.

22. With their angled ends face down, glue the lower-roof pieces to the angles of the front and back of the schoolhouse. Center the length of each roof piece over the assembly and butt its angled end to the upper side. Secure with eight #19 × ½" brads nailed through the pilot holes in the lower-roof pieces.

23. Glue the angled edges of the two upper-roof pieces together to form the roof peak. Glue the roof assembly to the top of the schoolhouse, centering its

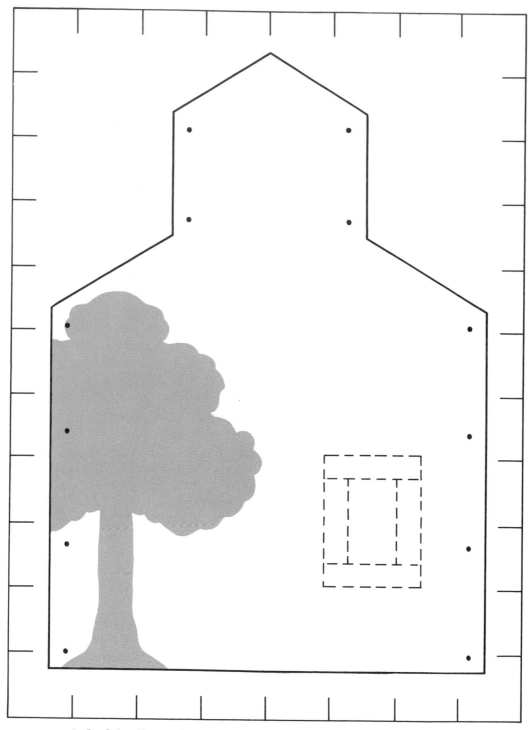

1–2. Schoolhouse, back. Each square equals 1". Enlarge and cut one.

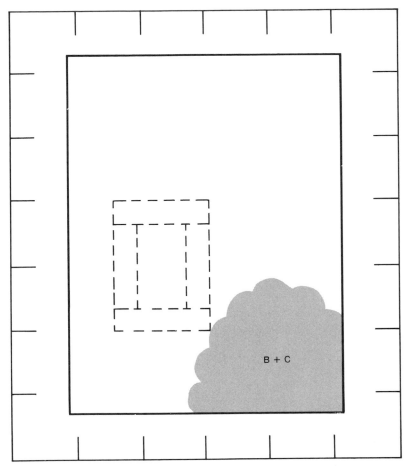

1–3. Schoolhouse, lower-left side. Each square equals 1″. Enlarge and cut one.

length on the schoolhouse. Secure with four #19 × ½″ brads nailed through the pilot holes in the roof assembly.

24. Glue the angled end of the chimney (1–11) to the middle of the roof peak.

25. Using the ⅜″ bit, drill a hole into the middle of the chimney's cut end and through the roof peak for the lamp pipe.

26. Glue the banner (1–5) to the front of the assembly, where indicated by the dashed line on 1–1.

27. For the support for bush A, cut a $1\frac{5}{8}$″ length from an ice-cream stick and glue it under the right window on the front of the assembly where indicated by the dashed lines on 1–1.

28. For the top step, cut a 3″ length from an ice cream stick and glue it to the bottom step (1–9), where indicated by the dashed line on the pattern. Glue the step assembly onto the base and to the front of the schoolhouse where indicated by the dashed line on 1–1.

29. Glue lengths of ice-cream sticks for the window and door frames where indicated by the dashed lines on patterns 1–1, 1–2, 1–3, and 1–4.

30. Glue the flat end of each hole plug to each corner on the underside of the base.

31. Paint the items described in a–g. Remember to paint $\frac{1}{16}$″ into the gluing outlines and extend the

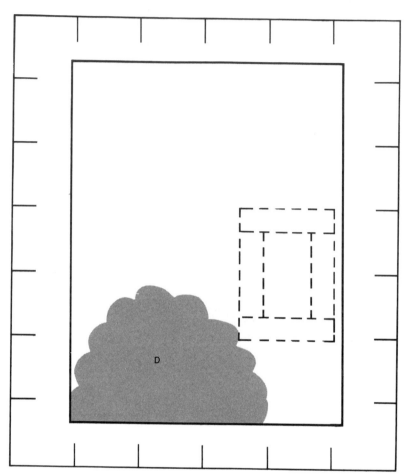

1–4. Schoolhouse, lower-right side. Each square equals 1". Enlarge and cut one.

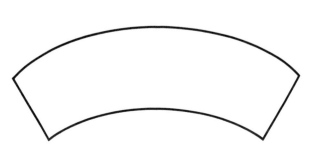

1–5. Banner (cut one).

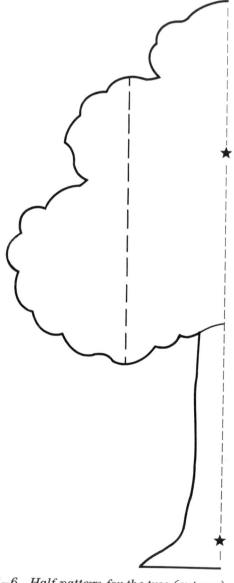

1–6. Half-pattern for the tree (cut one).

1–7. Small shrub (cut two).

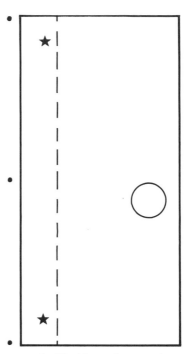

1–10. Door (cut one).

1–8. Large shrub (cut two).

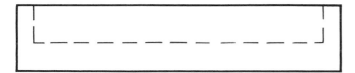

1–9. Bottom step (cut one).

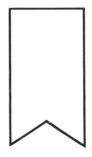

1–11. Chimney (cut one).

colors onto the edge surfaces. Don't paint the backs of the items unless instructed.

a. Paint the schoolhouse red. (Don't paint into the flagpole hole and don't paint the support for bush A on the front of the schoolhouse.)

b. Paint the window and door openings light grey, the steps dark grey, the chimney black, and the door and window frames ecru.

c. Paint all sides of the base medium-green.

d. Use medium-blue-grey to paint the banner and all exposed areas of the roofs.

e. Paint the tree trunk dark brown (1–6) and the tree top medium-green. Paint the back of the tree top up to the dashed line. Sponge dark green paint, using a 1 × 1″ sponge, in a ¼″- to ¾″-wide, irregular border on the front of the tree top. Continue sponging onto the back of the tree top, up to the dashed line.

f. Paint the shrubs (1–7 and 1–8) medium-green. Paint the backs of shrubs A, B, and C

1–12. Detail of schoolhouse showing girls' faces.

up to the dashed lines. (Don't paint the back of shrub D.) Sponge dark green paint on the fronts of the shrubs, as described for the tree top. (Don't sponge the bottom edges of the shrubs.) Continue sponging onto the backs of shrubs A, B, and C, up to the dashed lines.

g. Paint the door black. (Don't paint the whittled area on the back of the door.)

32. Glue the tree (1–6) to the back of the schoolhouse where indicated by the gluing outline on 1–2. Secure with two #19 × ½" brads nailed through the pilot holes in the tree.

33. Glue shrub A (1–7) to the support on the front of the schoolhouse, centering it left to right on the support.

34. Glue shrub B (1–7) onto shrub C (1–8) where indicated by the gluing outline on 1–8. Glue the shrub assembly to the lower-left side of the schoolhouse where indicated by the gluing outline on 1–3.

35. Glue shrub D (1–8) to the lower-right side of the schoolhouse where indicated by the gluing outline on 1–4.

36. Hammer the nail-head stud to the door where indicated by the circle on 1–10. Glue the whittled angle on the back of the door to the left side of the door opening where indicated by the outline of the gluing area on 1–1. Secure with two #10 × ½" brads nailed through the pilot holes in the door.

37. Apply the high-gloss finish. (Don't apply the finish to the gluing outlines in the window openings.)

38. Cut the 18-mm bead in half for the girls' heads. Paint the heads light pink. With the half-holes held vertically, paint the eyes black and the cheeks dark pink, as shown in 1–12. Use tacky glue to adhere ½" lengths of orange hair to one head and brown hair to the other. Use wood glue to adhere the heads to the gluing outlines on the front of the schoolhouse.

39. Adhere vinyl letters spelling SCHOOL to the banner (1–5), centering them from top to bottom and from left to right.

40. Insert the threaded lamp pipe into the chimney and though the base. Allow it to extend ¼" above the chimney, and secure the other end with the lock nut. Wire one end of the lamp wire to the socket. Feed the other end into the lamp pipe, extending from the chimney and out though the base. Screw the socket base onto the lamp pipe. Wire the plug to the other end of the lamp wire.

41. Use wood glue to adhere the end of the flagpole into the flagpole hole in the front of the schoolhouse.

42. Fit a light bulb into the socket and attach the lamp shade.

2. Schoolbooks Bookends

Schoolbooks Bookends

MATERIALS

- 18″ length of ½ × 5½ clear pine lattice
- 24″ length of 1 × 6 clear pine
- Drill bits: No. 61 (wire gauge) and 1⁄16″
- Four #4 × 1″ flat-head wood screws
- Four #18 × ¾″ wire brads
- Eight #18 × 1″ wire brads
- Four #18 × 1¼″ wire brads
- Acrylic paints: ecru, dark red, ultramarine, dark yellow, black, and medium-grey-blue
- High-gloss finish

Schoolbooks Bookends*

1. Cut two bookend bases (2–1) from 1 × 6 pine.

2. Cut two bookend sides (2–2) from ½ × 5½ pine lattice.

3. Referring to Table 1, cut two rectangles for each book.

Table 1. Lumber Sizes and Finished Dimensions for Each Book

Book	Use	Size
A	1 × 6 pine	1¾ × 2³⁄16″
B	½ × 5½ lattice	1¹⁵⁄16 × 2⅜″
C	1 × 6 pine	2⁵⁄16 × 3½″
D	1 × 6 pine	3 × 4¼″

*Refer to the General Directions for the techniques needed to complete this project.

4. Using the No. 61 bit, drill pilot holes through each bookend base, where indicated by the star on 2–1.

5. Using the 1⁄16″ bit, drill pilot holes through each bookend side, where indicated by the star on 2–2.

6. With the bottom edges even, glue the bookend sides to the bases. Secure by driving the screws through the pilot holes in the bookend sides.

7. Whittle and sand the edges of one long side of each book to form a spine.

8. Paint the book-page edges ecru.

9. Paint the book covers and spines, as listed in Table 2, extending the colors 1⁄16″ onto the page-edge surfaces.

Table 2. Paint Colors of the Books

Book	Color
A	Dark red
B	Ultramarine
C	Dark yellow
D	Dark red

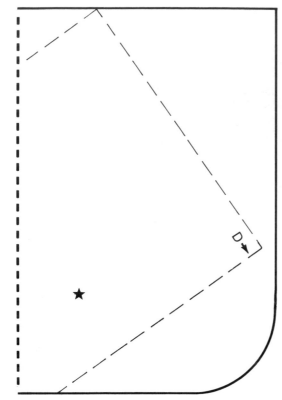

2—1. Half-pattern for the bookend's base (cut two).

2—2. Half-pattern for the bookend's side (cut two).

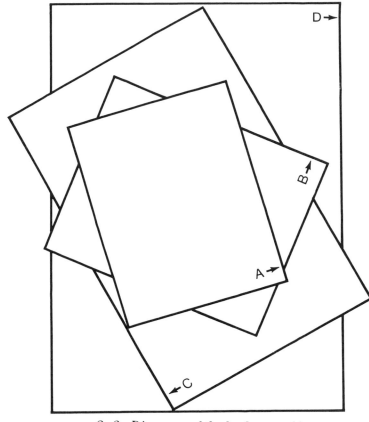

2–3. Diagram of the book assembly.

Table 3. Book Assembly Sequence and Brad Sizes to Use

Books	Brads
B* to A	#18 × ¾″
C* to B	#18 × 1″
D* to C	#18 × 1″

10. Outline the edges of the covers with black.

11. Paint the bookend assemblies medium-grey-blue.

12. Assemble the books in the sequence listed in Table 3. The brad sizes to use are also listed.

  a. Refer to 2–3 for the arrangement of the books. (The arrows on 2–3 indicate the directions in which the spines face.)

  b. Locate the middle of one face surface of each book that is starred in Table 3. Mark for a pilot hole ½″ above the middle mark towards the top of the book and another ½″ below the middle mark towards the bottom of the book.

  c. Using the No. 61 bit, drill pilot holes at the marks through each starred book.

  d. Following Table 3, use tacky glue to adhere book B to book A. Secure with two #18 × ¾″ brads nailed through the pilot holes in book B. Then adhere book C to book B, using the brad sizes recommended. Continue until the book assemblies are completed.

13. Refer to the dashed lines on 2–1 for the position of book D on the right side of a bookend base. (The arrow indicates the direction in which spine of book D faces.) Use tacky glue to adhere the book assemblies to the bookend bases. Secure each with two #18 × 1¼″ brads nailed through the pilot holes from the underside of the base.

14. Apply the high-gloss finish.

3. Apple Pencil Holder

Apple Pencil Holder

MATERIALS

- 3″ length of ¼ × 5¼ clear pine lattice
- 14″ length of 1 × 6 clear pine
- One 1⁹⁄₁₆″-long × ⁵⁄₁₆″-diameter wooden axle peg
- Drill bits: ³⁄₁₆″ and ⁵⁄₁₆″
- Spade bit: ⁵⁄₁₆″
- Acrylic paints: bright red, dark yellow, ochre, black, and medium-olive-green
- High-gloss finish

Apple Pencil Holder*

1. Cut two 7″ lengths of 1 × 6 pine, and glue the faces together to form one bonded piece with finished size of 7 × 5¼ × 1½″. Cut one apple (3–1) from the bonded wood.

2. Cut one apple leaf (3–2) from ¼ × 5¼ pine lattice.

3. Using the ⁵⁄₁₆″ bit, drill a ¼″-deep peg hole into the middle-top surface of the apple where indicated by the large arrow on 3–1.

4. On the top surface of the apple, mark ³⁄₈″ from the middle of one edge (now the back) for the leaf-stem hole. Using the ³⁄₁₆″ bit, drill a ¼″-deep hole. (The shank of the axle peg, used for the stem, will extend 1⁵⁄₁₆″ from the hole after assembly.)

5. On the top surface of the apple, where indicated by the small arrows on 3–1, mark for four pairs of pencil holes. Space each pair of holes ³⁄₈″ from the front and back edges. Using the ⁵⁄₁₆″ spade bit, drill 3″-deep holes.

6. Paint the apple bright red. Paint into the pencil holes, but not into the peg or leaf-stem holes.

7. Sponge a dark yellow highlight, as shown in the color photograph section, on the right-side edge of the apple, using a 2 × 2″ sponge. Continue sponging slightly onto the front, back, and top surfaces, allowing some bright red to show through.

8. Using a 2 × 2″ sponge, sponge ochre over the highlight and allow some dark yellow and bright red to show through.

9. Paint the axle peg black, leaving the bottom ¼″ of the shank unpainted.

10. Paint the leaf medium-olive green, leaving the bottom ¼″ of the stem unpainted.

11. Glue the axle peg into the peg hole and the leaf stem into the stem hole.

12. Apply the high-gloss finish.

---

*Refer to the General Directions for the techniques needed to complete this project.

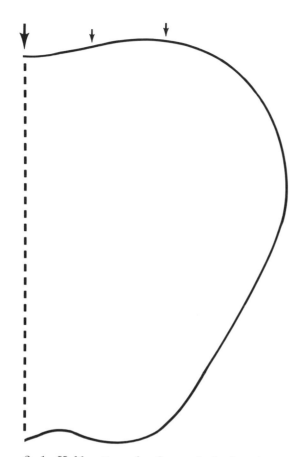

3–2. Apple leaf (cut one).

3–1. Half-pattern for the apple (cut one).

4. Country-Cat Shelf Decoration

Country-Cat Shelf Decoration

4–1 (a). Cat's body, top. Assemble the three patterns (a, b, c) on the dotted lines and cut one.

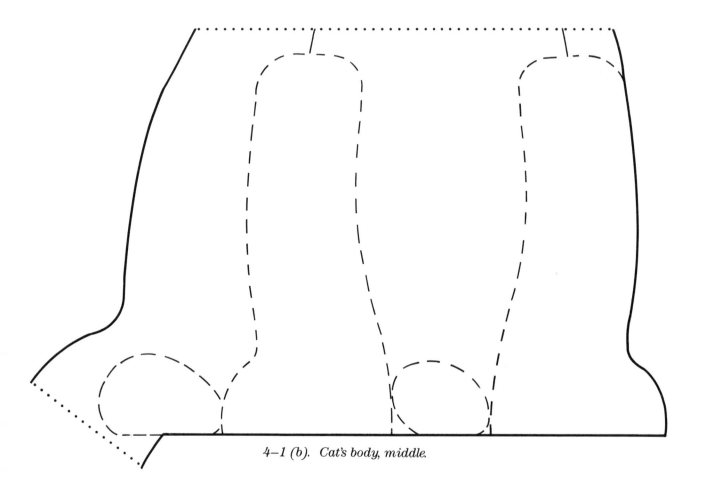

4–1 (b). Cat's body, middle.

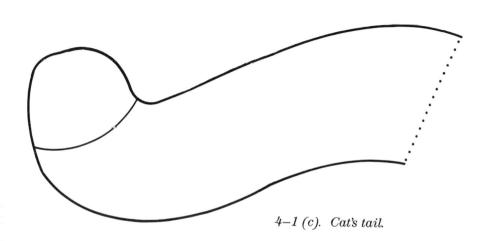

4–1 (c). Cat's tail.

MATERIALS

- 3″ length of ¼ × 5¼ clear pine lattice
- 3″ length of ½ × 5½ clear pine lattice
- 24″ length of 1 × 12 clear pine
- One white, 8-mm, regular-hole, round wood bead
- Two white, 10-mm, regular-hole, round wood beads
- Drill bit: ⁵⁄₆₄″
- Eighteen 2¾″-long black brush bristles
- Acrylic paint: white, light pink, light pinkish-brown, dark red-brown, dark yellow, and black
- High-gloss finish

Country-Cat Shelf Decoration*

1. Cut one body (4–1) and two front legs (4–2) from 1 × 12 pine. The pattern for the front leg (4–2) shows the orientation of the right front leg; the left front leg is a mirror image.

2. Cut two front paws (4–3), one left back paw (4–4), and one right back paw (4–5) from ½ × 5½ pine lattice. The pattern for the front paw (4–3) shows the orientation of the left front paw; the right front paw is a mirror image.

3. Cut one nose (4–6) and two cheeks (4–7) from ¼ × 5¼ pine lattice.

4. Using the ⁵⁄₆₄″ bit, drill ¼″-deep whisker holes, where indicated by the stars on 4–1, angling the bit slightly towards the middle back of the head.

5. Whittle and sand to contour the front edges of the body (4–1), except at the bottom and left, where the feet and paws will be glued. Contour the front edges of the legs (4–2), paws (4–3, 4–4, and 4–5), nose (4–6) and cheeks (4–7). Define the toes on the paws by whittling.

6. Split a 10-mm bead in half for the eyes. With the half-holes held horizontal, glue the eyes to the head, where indicated by the large dots on 4–1.

7. Glue the nose (4–6) and cheeks (4–7) to the head where indicated by the dashed lines on 4–1.

*Refer to the General Directions for the techniques needed to complete this project.

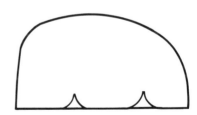

4–2. Cat's front leg (cut two).

4–3. Cat's front paw (cut two).

4–4. Cat's left back paw (cut one).

4–5. Cat's right back paw (cut one).

8. Split the remaining 10-mm bead in half for the muzzle. With the half-holes held horizontal, glue the muzzle to the head where indicated by the small circles on 4–1.

9. Split the 8-mm bead in half for the tongue. (Discard one-half.) With the half-holes angled, as shown by the dashed line, glue the tongue to the head where indicated by the small dot on 4–1.

10. Glue the front legs (4–2) to the body, where indicated by the dashed lines on 4–1.

11. Glue the left (4–4) and right (4–5) back paws to the body, where indicated by the dashed lines on 4–1.

12. Glue the front paws (4–3) to the front legs where indicated by the dashed line on 4–2.

13. As shown in the opening photograph, use white to paint the inner ears, face, muzzle, chest, paws, inner half of the cheeks and front legs, and tip of the tail on the front and back of the assembly. Extend all colors onto the edge surfaces. Paint the nose and tongue light pink.

14. Use light pinkish-brown to paint the remainder of the front and the back. Paint into the white areas, using a dry-brush technique. To do this, dip the brush into the light pinkish-brown and then wipe it on paper towels to remove the excess paint. Using short strokes, brush the paint lightly into all of the white areas, except the inner ears.

15. Using a 1 × 1″ sponge, sponge dark red-brown paint on the forehead, the side edges of the cheeks, and the edge surfaces of the body, legs, and tail. Allow some light pinkish-brown to show through.

16. Referring to the opening photograph and 4–8, use the dry-brush technique (see step 14) with dark red-brown paint to paint the tabby stripes and to define the tail on the back. Using overlapping, short, light brush strokes, brush slightly into the light red-brown and white areas.

17. Paint the eyes dark yellow and the eye outlines and pupils black.

18. Apply the high-gloss finish only to the eyes and tongue.

19. Gather nine brush bristles together, and hold them close to one end. Dip that end into tacky glue, and insert it into one of the whisker holes. Repeat for the other whisker hole.

4–6. Cat's nose (cut one).

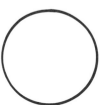

4–7. Cat's cheek (cut two).

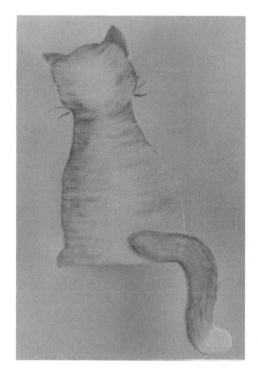

4–8. Back view of the cat.

5. Sheep Corner Shelf

Sheep Corner Shelf

MATERIALS

- 12″ length of ¼ × 5¼ clear pine lattice
- 10″ length of ½ × 5½ clear pine lattice
- 17″ length of 1 × 12 clear pine
- One white, 10-mm, regular-hole, round wood bead
- Drill bits: No. 61 (wire gauge), ¹⁄₁₆″, and ³⁄₁₆″ (optional)
- Six #6 × 1½″ flat-head wood screws
- Four #19 × ½″ wire brads
- Two #17 × ⅞″ wire brads
- Acrylic paints: white, black, light yellow-green, and light red-brown
- Satin finish

Sheep Corner Shelf*

1. Cut one front half (5–1) and one rear half (5–2) body from 1 × 12 pine.

2. Cut one shelf (5–3) and one head (5–4) from ½ × 5½ pine lattice.

3. Cut two ears (5–5), one tail (5–6), and two grasses (5–7) from ¼ × 5¼ pine lattice. The pattern for the grass (5–7) shows the orientation for the grass under the sheep's right legs; the grass under the sheep's left legs is a mirror image.

4. Using the No. 61 bit, drill pilot holes through the grasses (5–7) where indicated by the stars on the pattern.

---

*Refer to the General Directions for the techniques needed to complete this project.

5. Using the ¹⁄₁₆″ bit, drill pilot holes through the front and rear halves of the body, where indicated by the stars on 5–1 and 5–2.

6. Using the ¹⁄₁₆″ bit, drill pilot holes through the head where indicated by the stars on 5–4.

7. (Optional.) For hanging the shelf on a wall, use the ³⁄₁₆″ bit to drill holes through the front and rear halves of the body where indicated by the dots on 5–1 and 5–2. After finishing, secure the shelf to the wall with molly or toggle bolts. The holes are not necessary if the shelf is to stand on a counter top.

8. Lap the front half of the body (5–1) over the rear-edge surface of the back half of the body (5–2). The edges should be flush. Drill through the pilot holes in the front half into the edge surface of the rear half. Glue and secure with two screws.

9. Glue the shelf (5–3) centered over the pilot holes in the body assembly. Use the ¹⁄₁₆″ bit to drill through the pilot holes in the body and into the rear edge of the shelf. Secure the shelf with four screws.

10. Glue the head (5–4) to the body, where indicated by the dashed line on 5–1, and secure with two #17 × ⅞″ brads nailed through the pilot holes in the head.

Red Barn Wall Clock (pp. 92–97).

Carrot-Bunch Utensil Rack (pp. 104–105); Sweet-Pepper Napkin Holder (pp. 98–99); Eggplant Paper-Towel Dispenser (pp. 100–103).

A

Clockwise from center: Pumpkin-Leaf Trivet (pp. 114–115); Strawberry Napkin Ring (pp. 108–109); Watermelon Place Mat (pp. 106–107); Wheelbarrow Condiment Holder (pp. 110–113).

Hen Measuring Spoon and Cup Rack (pp. 116–121).

Apple Harvest Refrigerator Magnets (pp. 122–125).

Schoolbooks Bookends (pp. 23–25); Apple Pencil Holder (pp. 26–27); Schoolhouse Desk Lamp (pp. 15–22).

Country-Cat Shelf Decoration (pp. 28–31).

Sheep Corner Shelf (pp. 32–36).

*Top left: Potted-Flowers Basket
(pp. 37–41). Top right: Pig-
Silhouette Message Board
(pp. 48–49). Left: Farmhouse Key
Caddy and Country-Cat Key Chains
(pp. 42–47).*

Right: Rooster Pull Toy (pp. 50–52). Bottom: Shaker Peg Shelf (pp. 53–54) with Farm-Scene Knickknacks (pp. 55–59) and Welcome Sign (pp. 60–61).

E

Checkered Step Stool (pp. 62–64);
Sunflower Plant Sticks (pp. 65–66);
Monarch Butterfly Plant Stick (pp.
67–68).

Sheep Plant Stand (pp. 69–74).

F

Top: Checkerboard Serving Tray and Heart Checkers (pp. 75–76); Country Heart Coasters and Caddy (pp. 77–78).

Right: Vegetable Ornaments and Garden Rake Display Rack (pp. 79–83).

G

Cow Wind Chimes (pp. 84–85).

Horse Weather Vane (pp. 86–89);
Decorative Watermelon Slices (pp. 90–91).

H

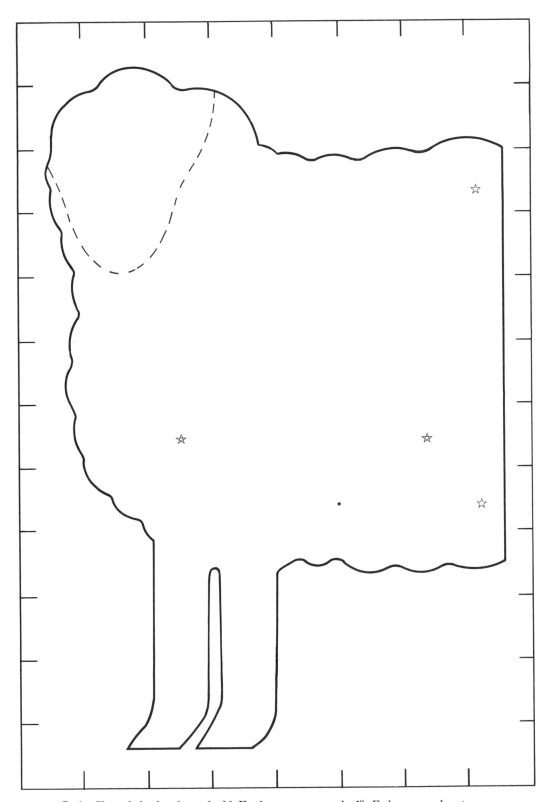

5–1. Sheep's body, front half. Each square equals 1". Enlarge and cut one.

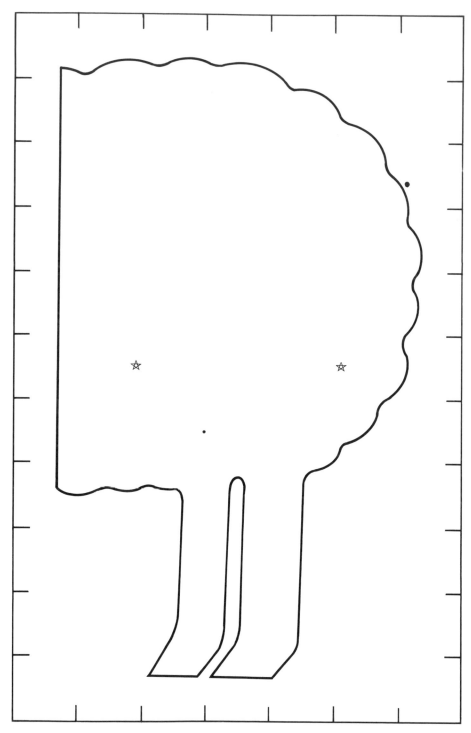

5–2. *Sheep's body, rear half. Each square equals 1". Enlarge and cut one.*

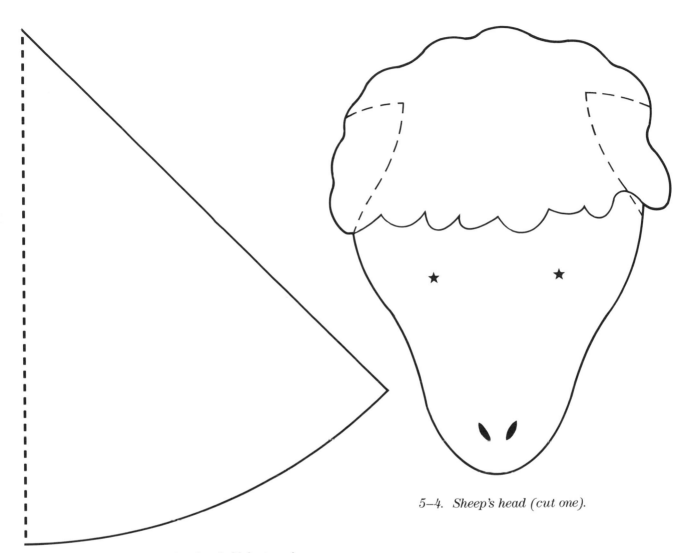

5–4. *Sheep's head (cut one).*

5–3. *Half-pattern for the shelf (cut one).*

11. Split the 10-mm bead in half for the eyes. With the half-holes held horizontal, glue the eyes to the head on top of the brad heads.

12. Glue the ears (5–5) to the head where indicated by the dashed lines on 5–4.

13. Align the dot at the top of the tail (5–6) with the dot on the rear half of the body (5–2). Whittle the underside of the tail to the same contours as the back-edge surface of the body and then adhere with glue.

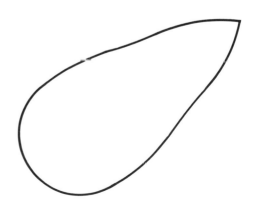

5–5. *Sheep's ear (cut two).*

14. Glue the grasses (5–7) to the bottoms of the legs. Center the pilot holes in the grasses under each leg, and align the straight edge of each grass with the backs of the legs. Secure each with two #19 × ½″ brads nailed through the pilot holes in the grass.

15. Use white to paint the body, shelf, tail, forehead, nostrils, and ears. Paint the face and legs black. Paint the grasses light yellow-green.

16. Use black to paint a ¼″-diameter circle in the middle of each eye for the pupil. Around the pupil, paint a ⅛″ band of light red-brown, then a ³⁄₃₂″ band of white, and finally a ¹⁄₁₆″ band of black at the base of the eye. Use white to highlight each pupil at 3 o'clock.

17. Use a 1 × 1″ sponge to dab a thick coat of white paint with dense, raised areas onto the dry paint of the forehead.

18. Apply the satin finish.

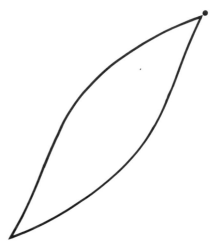

5–6. Sheep's tail (cut one).

5–7. Grass (cut two).

6. Potted-Flowers Basket

MATERIALS

- 12 × 48″ rectangle of ¼″ birch plywood
- 98″ length of ¼ × 1⅛ clear pine lattice
- 12″ length of ½ × 5½ clear pine lattice
- 12″ length of 1 × 8 clear pine
- 12″ length of ⅝″ dowelling
- Three 25-mm, large-hole, round wood beads
- Drill bits: No. 61 (wire gauge) and 1⁄16″
- Two #4 × ¾″ flat-head wood screws
- Twenty-two #19 × ½″ wire brads
- Eight #18 × ¾″ wire brads
- Two #18 × ⅞″ wire brads
- Pencil compass
- Acrylic paints: dark orange, medium-olive-green, light pink, dark green, and dark yellow
- High-gloss and satin finishes

Potted-Flowers Basket

Potted Flowers Basket*

1. Cut two basket sides (6–1) from ½ × 5½ pine lattice.

2. Cut two flowerpots (6–2) from 1 × 8 pine. Transfer the outline of the tinted (gluing) area onto the front of each flowerpot.

3. Cut two large leaves (6–3), six small leaves (6–4), and six flowers (6–5) from ¼″ plywood. The pattern shows the orientation of the left small leaves (6–4); the right small leaves are mirror images.

4. Cut nine 10½″ lengths of ¼ × 1⅛ pine lattice for the side and bottom slats.

5. Using the No. 61 bit, drill pilot holes through the basket sides (6–1) and the large leaves (6–3) where indicated by the small stars on the patterns.

6. At both ends of each slat, mark for a pilot hole centered ³⁄16″ from the cut end. Using the No. 61 bit, drill pilot holes through the slats.

*Refer to the General Directions for the techniques needed to complete this project.

7. Using the 1⁄16″ bit, drill holes through the large leaves where indicated by the large star on 6–3.

8. Glue a basket side (6–1) to the back of each flowerpot where indicated by the dashed line on 6–2. Secure with #18 × ¾″ brads nailed into the pilot holes in the basket sides.

9. Paint the flowerpots dark orange, omitting the upper-back edges of the pots and painting 1⁄16″ into the gluing outlines on the fronts of the pots. (Don't paint the sides of the baskets.)

10. Glue and nail the side slats (using #19 × ½″ brads) to the basket sides. Position the top slats flush with the tops of the basket sides and the bottom slats flush with the bottoms of the flowerpots. Butt all slats to the backs of the flowerpots. Center the middle slats between the top and bottom slats.

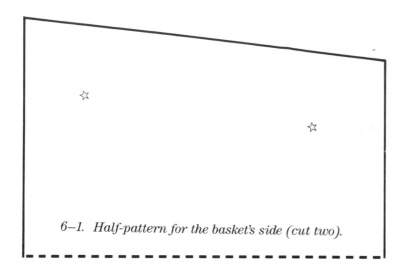

6–1. *Half-pattern for the basket's side (cut two).*

6–2. *Flowerpot (cut two).*

6–3. Half-pattern for the large leaf (cut two).

11. Glue and nail the bottom slats (using #19 × ½″ brads) to the bottoms of the basket sides. Butt the left and right slats to the bottom-side slats and the backs of the flowerpots. Center the middle slat between the left and right slats.

12. Glue the large leaves (6–3) to the middle backs of the flowerpots, with their bottom edges butted to

the tops of the basket sides. Secure with #18 × ¾″ brads nailed through the bottom-two pilot holes in each large leaf.

13. Measure between the pilot holes in the upper midpoints of the large leaves to determine the handle's length (approximately 10¼″). Cut the dowelling to that length. Using the ⅟₁₆″ bit, drill ¼″-

deep pilot holes into the middle of each end of the dowelling. Glue and secure the handle between the large leaves, using the two screws.

14. Mark the middle front of four small leaves (6–4) as left leaves. Flop the other two small leaves over, and mark them as right leaves. Using the pencil compass, describe a ¾″-diameter circle on the middle front and middle back of each small leaf. Omitting the circles, paint all sides of the leaves medium-olive-green.

15. Describe a ½″-diameter circle on the middle front and a ¾″-diameter circle on the middle back of each flower (6–5). Omitting the circles, paint all sides of the flowers light pink.

16. Glue the backs of the flowers to the fronts of the small leaves, aligning the flowers on the leaves, as shown in 6–6.

17. Using the No. 61 bit, drill a pilot hole through the middle of each leaf-flower assembly.

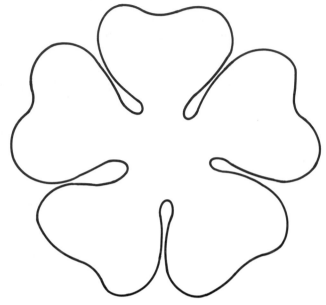

6–5. Flower (cut six).

6–4. Small leaf (cut six).

18. On each side of the basket, position a right leaf-flower assembly at the upper right and a left leaf-flower assembly at the lower left of the large leaf, as shown in 6–6. Trace the outlines of the small leaves onto the large leaves.

19. Working 1/16" into the outlined areas, use dark green to paint all sides of the large leaves.

20. Glue the leaf-flower assemblies to the large leaves, and secure with #19 × 1/2" brads nailed through the pilot holes.

21. Position the remaining two left leaf-flower assemblies over the gluing outlines on the flowerpots. Glue and secure, using #18 × 7/8" brads nailed through the pilot holes.

22. Split the three 25-mm beads in half, and glue them to the centers of the flowers. Fill the half-holes with paste wood filler, allow to dry, and sand smooth.

23. Paint the flower centers dark yellow.

24. Apply the high-gloss finish to all painted surfaces and the satin finish to the unpainted surfaces.

6–6. Arrangement of the leaf-flower assemblies.

7. Farmhouse Key Caddy and Country-Cat Key Chains

Left: *Farmhouse Key Caddy;* right: *Country-Cat Key Chains*

MATERIALS

- 10 × 11″ rectangle of ¼″ birch plywood
- 26″ length of ¼ × 5¼ clear pine lattice
- 12″ length of 1 × 1 clear pine
- One 1⁹⁄₁₆″-long × ⁵⁄₁₆″-diameter wooden axle peg
- Drill bits: No. 61 (wire gauge) and ¹⁄₁₆″
- Twenty #19 × ½″ wire brads
- One 2½″-long sawtooth hanger, with supplied brads
- Five ½″-long × ¼″-diameter screw eyes
- One 6½-mm, white, flat nail-head stud
- Five brass cup hooks
- Small amount of white decorative adhesive covering
- Five 4⅝″-long beaded key chains, with fasteners
- Acrylic paints: medium-taupe, bright red, black (B), white (W), light yellow-green, dark green, dark blue-grey, pale yellow, dark grey, dark taupe, light pink, medium-orange, dark yellow, light apricot (LA), pale grey (PG), and light red-brown (LRB)
- High-gloss finish

Farmhouse Key Caddy*

1. Cut two 1″ lengths from the 12″ length of 1 × 1 pine for the bush supports. The remaining 10″ length is the base. Transfer the painting patterns for the sidewalk (7–1 and 7–2) onto the top and front of the base. Transfer the edge of the tinted (gluing) area in 7–2 onto the front of the base.

2. Cut two ½ × 6⅝″ rectangles from ¼″ plywood for the roof eaves.

3. Cut one farmhouse (7–3) from ¼″ plywood.

4. Cut two roof trims (7–4) and two bushes (7–5) from ¼ × 5¼ pine lattice. The bush pattern (7–5) shows the orientation of the left bush; the right bush is a mirror image. Transfer the outline of the tinted (gluing) area on 7–5 onto the backs of the bushes.

5. Draw a line ⅜″ from and parallel with one long side of the bottom of the base. Using the ¹⁄₁₆″ bit, drill ¼″-deep pilot holes on the line, where indicated by the arrows on 7–2.

---

*Refer to the General Directions for the techniques needed to complete this project.

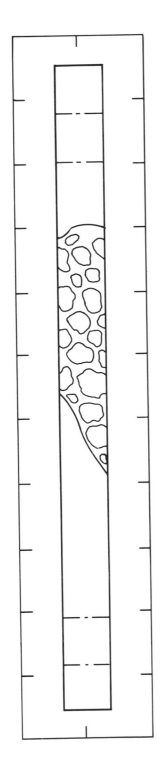

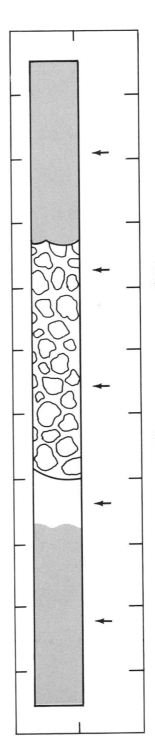

7–1. Painting pattern for the base top. Each square equals 1". Enlarge and transfer onto the top of the base.

7–2. Painting pattern for the base front. Each square equals 1". Enlarge and transfer onto the front of the base.

7–3. Farmhouse. Each square equals 1". Enlarge and cut one.

44

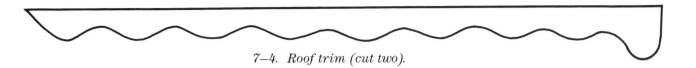

7–4. Roof trim (cut two).

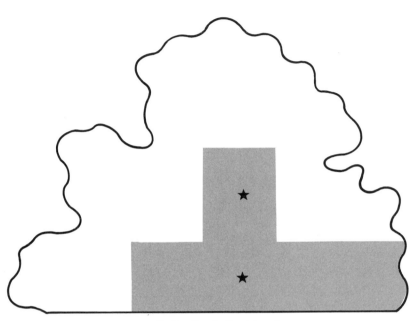

7–5. Bush (cut two).

6. Using the No. 61 bit, drill pilot holes through the farmhouse (7–3) and the bushes (7–5), where indicated by the stars on the patterns.

7. Glue the back of the base to the farmhouse (7–3) where indicated by the dashed line on 7–3. Secure with four brads nailed through the pilot holes in the farmhouse.

8. Glue the bush supports to the front of the farmhouse (7–3) where indicated by the dashed lines on 7–3. Secure with eight brads nailed through the pilot holes in the farmhouse.

9. Glue one long edge of each roof eave to the front of the farmhouse where indicated by the dashed lines on 7–3. Secure with brads nailed through the pilot holes in the farmhouse.

10. Glue the long straight edges of the roof trims (7–4) under the eaves, aligning the roof trims with the fronts of the eaves.

11. Trim the shank of the axle peg to ½″, and glue it to the ends of the eaves and the front of the roof's peak.

12. Paint the items described in a–j. Remember to paint ¹⁄₁₆″ into the gluing outlines and extend the colors onto the edge surfaces. Don't paint the backs of the items unless instructed.
  - **a.** Paint the front of the farmhouse medium-taupe.
  - **b.** Use bright red to paint the door, windowbox, and chimney.
  - **c.** Use black to paint all sides of the roof eaves, the axle peg, the attic window, and the outlines of the chimney's bricks. Continue the chimney's bricks onto the edge surfaces.
  - **d.** Paint the roof trims and the attic window's shutters white.
  - **e.** Paint the curtains dark blue-grey and inside the window pale yellow.

f. Use light yellow-green to paint the windowbox foliage and the wreath.

g. Paint all sides of the bushes light yellow-green. Sponge dark green paint, using a 1 × 1″ sponge, in a ¼- to 1″-wide, irregular border on the fronts of the bushes, as shown in the color section.

h. Use light yellow-green to paint the top, front, bottom, and sides of the base, and the tops and sides of the bush supports. (Don't paint the fronts of the bush supports.)

i. Paint the sidewalk dark grey and the sidewalk flagstones dark taupe.

j. As shown in the color photograph, overpaint dots of light pink, medium-orange, and dark yellow in various sizes on the windowbox foliage and the wreath.

13. With their bottom edges even, glue the bushes to the front of the base and the bush supports where indicated by the outlines of the gluing areas on 7–2 and 7–5. Secure with two brads nailed through the pilot holes in each bush.

14. Paint the back of the assembly black.

15. Apply the high-gloss finish.

16. Cut ⅛″-wide strips of white decorative adhesive covering for the door trim, downstairs window trim, and attic windowsill. Adhere the strips where indicated on 7–3. Use a craft knife to mitre corners and to trim around the windowbox planting.

17. Hammer the nail-head stud to the door where indicated by the circle on 7–3.

18. Thread the cup hooks into the pilot holes in the bottom of the base, making sure that they face forwards.

19. Nail the sawtooth hanger to the back of the farmhouse, centered 1⅜″ below the roof peak.

Country Cat Key Chains

1. Cut five cats (7–6) and five tails (7–7) from ¼ × 5¼ pine lattice.

2. Glue the tails (7–7) to the fronts of the cats where indicated by the dashed line on 7–6.

3. Paint the cats' bodies and ears according to the Table. Refer to the Materials list for the paint color

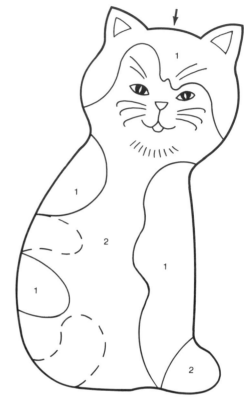

7–6. *Cat (cut five).*

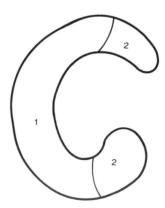

7–7. *Cat's tail (cut five).*

codes. Extend all colors onto the edge surfaces, and paint the backs of the cats as shown on 7–8.

Table: Paint Colors for Each Cat

Cat	Area 1	Area 2	Ears
A. White-grey	W	PG	LA
B. Brown-white	LRB	W	LA
C. Grey-black	PG	B	B
D. Black-white	B	W	LA
E. Black-brown	B	LRB	LA

4. Paint the noses and tongues light apricot. Paint the eye outlines and pupils black, the eye slits white, and the area around the pupils medium-orange. (There is no eye outline for cat C, since the area around the eyes is painted black.)

5. Paint the balance of each face as follows:
  a. Use black to paint the face details on cats A and B.
  b. Use black to paint the face details on cats D and E, with the exception of the left eyebrow whiskers, which are to be painted white.
  c. Use white to paint the face details on cat C, with the exception of the left eyebrow whiskers, which are to be painted black.

6. Apply the high-gloss finish.

7. Use an ice pick to make a ⅛″-deep pilot hole in each cat where indicated by the arrow on 7–6. Thread the screw eyes into the pilot holes. Make sure that the holes are at right angles to the bodies.

8. Insert a beaded key chain through each screw eye and fasten.

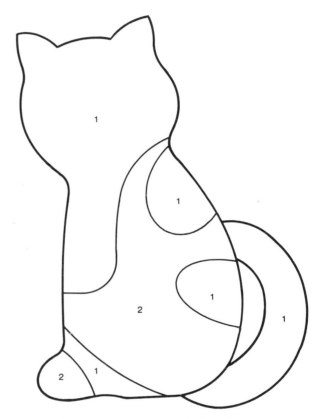

7–8. Rear view of the cat.

8. Pig-Silhouette Message Board

Pig-Silhouette Message Board

MATERIALS

- 11 × 15″ rectangle of ¼″ birch plywood
- 19″ length of 1 × 1 clear pine
- Drill bits: ⁵⁄₆₄″ and ⁷⁄₃₂″
- Four #19 × ½″ wire brads
- 6½″ length of thread-covered floral wire
- Oil-base paint: flat black
- Oil-base satin finish

Pig-Silhouette Message Board*

1. Cut one body (8–1) and two ears (8–2) from ¼″ plywood.

2. Cut the 19″ length of 1 × 1 pine in half for the base.

3. Using the ⁷⁄₃₂″ bit, drill a hole through the head for the eye where indicated by the star on 8–1.

4. Using the ⁵⁄₆₄″ bit, drill a ¼″-deep tail hole where indicated by the arrow on 8–1.

5. Glue the ears (8–2) to the sides of the head where indicated by the dashed lines on 8–1. Follow the heavy dashed line for the right ear and the light dashed line for the left ear.

6. Position the pig's hooves on a base-half so that the tip of its front hoof is 1¼″ from the front edge of the base and the bottom edges of the hooves align with the bottom of the base-half. Glue and nail the hooves to the base-half, where indicated by the dots on 8–1.

7. Glue the remaining base-half to the other side of the hooves, making sure that all edges align.

8. Coil the floral wire loosely around a pencil, and use tacky glue to adhere one end of the wire into the tail hole.

9. Paint the assembly black.

10. Apply the satin finish to the base only.

11. Wipe with a damp, soft cloth or sponge to remove chalk marks.

---

*Refer to the General Directions for the techniques needed to complete this project.

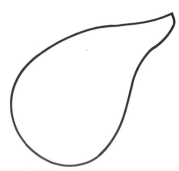

8–2. Pig's ear (cut two).

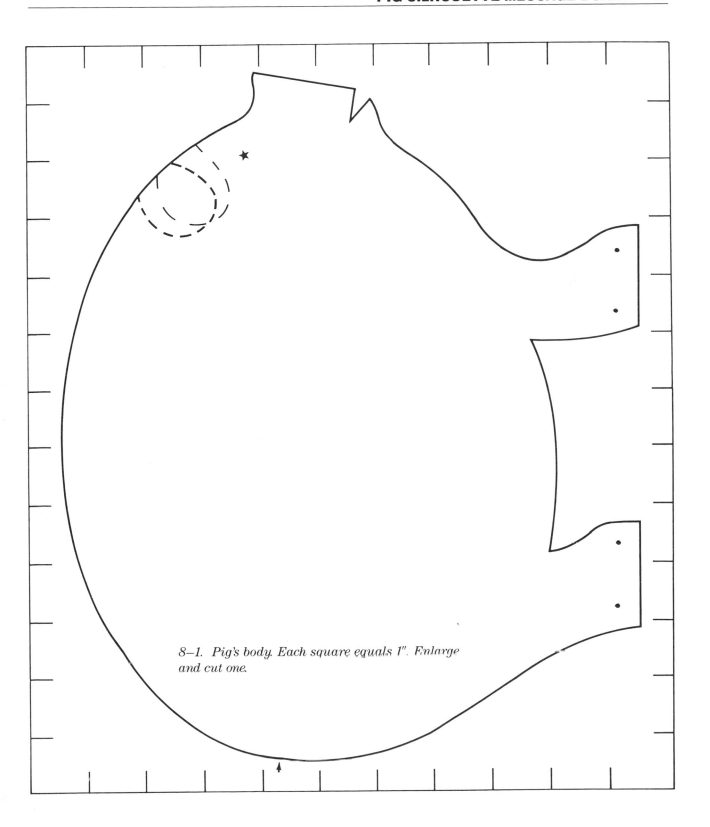

8–1. Pig's body. Each square equals 1". Enlarge and cut one.

9. Rooster Pull Toy

Rooster Pull Toy

MATERIALS

- 12″ length of ¼ × 5¼ clear pine lattice
- 10″ length of 1 × 6 clear pine
- 14″ length of 1 × 12 clear pine
- Four 1⁷⁄₁₆″-long × ⅜″-diameter wooden axle pegs
- One 1½″-diameter wooden wheel (¼″ axle hole)
- Four 2½″-diameter wooden wheels (⅜″ axle hole)
- One white, 10-mm, regular-hole, round wood bead
- Drill bits: ¹⁄₁₆″, ³⁄₁₆″, and ⅜″
- Three #6 × 1½″ flat-head wood screws
- Four ⅜″ flat washers
- 42″-long, red, flat-woven boot lace
- Acrylic paint: white, bright red, dark yellow, black, and light yellow-green
- High-gloss finish

Rooster*

1. Cut one body (9–1) from 1 × 12 pine.

2. Cut two wings (9–2) and two leg feathers (9–3) from ¼ × 5¼ pine lattice.

3. Glue the wings (9–2) and the leg feathers (9–3) to the sides of the body, where indicated by the dashed lines on 9–1.

4. Split the 10-mm bead in half for the eyes. With the half-holes angled as shown by the dashed lines on 9–1, glue the eyes to the sides of the head where indicated by the dot on the pattern.

---

*Refer to the General Directions for the techniques needed to complete this project.

5. Use white to paint the body, wings, and leg feathers. Paint the comb and wattles bright red and the beak dark yellow.

6. Paint the eyes black, and use white to highlight the right eye at 3 o'clock and the left eye at 9 o'clock.

Platform

1. Cut a 5¼ × 9¼″ rectangle from 1 × 6 pine for the platform.

2. In the middle of the edge surface of one short side of the platform, mark for the pull hole. (This is the front of the platform.) Using the ³⁄₁₆″ bit, drill a 1″-deep hole.

3. On the edge surface of each long side, mark for two axle-peg holes, 1⅞″ from the front and 1⅝″ from the back, and centered from top to bottom. Using the ⁵⁄₁₆″ bit, drill ⅜″-deep holes. (The shank of each axle peg should extend 1¹⁄₁₆″ from the hole to allow for the thickness of the washer and the wheel as well as ¹⁄₁₆″ of play.)

4. Mark for three pilot holes on the top of the platform. Draw a line (A) down the middle of the

9–1. *Rooster's body. Each square equals 1".*
Enlarge and cut one.

platform's length and a line (B) across the middle of the width. Where the lines cross, mark for the middle pilot hole. On line A, mark 1⅜" at either side of the central mark for the two remaining pilot holes. Using the ¹⁄₁₆" bit, drill holes through the platform.

5. Insert the screws from the underside of the platform so that their tips extend slightly above the top surface. Place the rooster on the platform, centering its base over the screw tips and pressing slightly to make indentations in the bottom of its base. Remove the screws from the platform.

6. Using the ¹⁄₁₆" bit, drill three ¾"-deep pilot holes into the rooster's base at each indentation.

7. Paint the platform light yellow-green. Use black to paint the 1½"-diameter wheel used for the pull

knob and the four 2½"-diameter wheels. Paint the axle-peg caps bright red.

8. Secure the rooster to the platform with the screws driven from the underside of the platform.

9. Apply the high-gloss finish to the entire assembly, pull knob, 2½"-diameter wheels, and axle-peg caps.

10. To attach each wheel, apply a small amount of glue into an axle-peg hole in the platform. Insert an axle peg through the hole in a wheel, through a washer, and then into the glued axle-peg hole in the platform. The wheels should be able to spin freely.

11. Use tacky glue to adhere one end of the boot lace into the pull hole in the platform. Knot the lacing 3" from the free end. Draw the free end through the hole in the pull knob. Knot the free end close to the knob, and trim the end close to the knot.

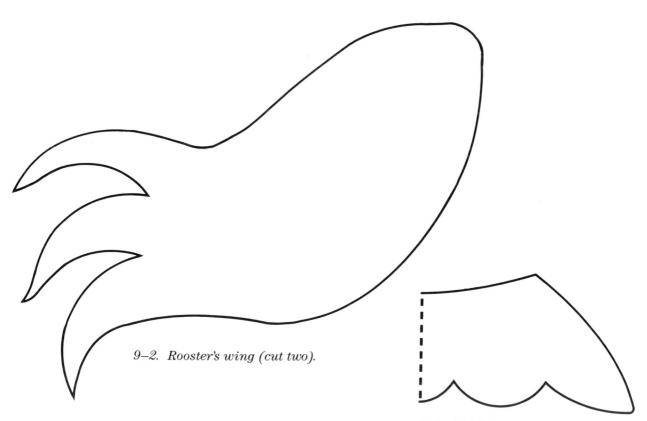

9–2. Rooster's wing (cut two).

9–3. Half-pattern for the rooster's leg feathers (cut two).

10. Shaker Peg Shelf

MATERIALS

- 47″ length of ½ × 3½ clear pine lattice
- 45″ length of ½ × 5½ clear pine lattice
- Five 2½″-long Shaker pegs (Trim the shanks to ¼″ long, if necessary.)
- Drill bits: No. 61 (wire gauge), ⅟₁₆″, and ²³⁄₆₄″ (Note: Use a bit that matches the diameter of the Shaker-peg shank.)
- Four #4 × 1″ flat-head wood screws
- Nineteen #18 × 1¼″ wire brads
- Two 1½″-long sawtooth hangers, with supplied brads
- Acrylic paint: medium-grey-blue
- Satin finish

Shaker Peg Shelf

Shaker Peg Shelf*

1. Cut a 15½″ length of ½ × 5½ pine lattice for the top shelf. Cut the front corners following 10–1.

2. Cut two 15½″ lengths of ½ × 3½ pine lattice for the shelf sides. Round the bottom front corners following 10–1.

3. Draw a line ¾″ from and parallel with each short side of the top shelf. Measuring from the back edge, mark the following two points on each line: ½″ and 2⅞″. Using the ⅟₁₆″ bit, drill pilot holes through the top shelf at each mark.

4. Draw another line ¼″ from and parallel with the back edge of the top shelf. On the line, mark 2″ from each short side and then locate and mark the middle of the length. Using the No. 61 bit, drill pilot holes through the top shelf at each mark.

5. Draw a line ¼″ from and parallel with the back edge of each shelf side. Measuring from the top edge, mark these points on each line: ½″, 2¾″, 5″,

---

*Refer to the General Directions for the techniques needed to complete this project.

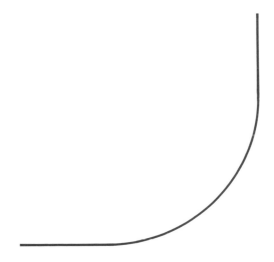

10–1. Pattern for top shelf's front corners and the shelf sides' bottom-front corners.

5¾″, 6½″, 8¾″, and 11″. Using the No. 61 bit, drill pilot holes through the shelf sides at each mark.

6. Have the straight back edges of the top shelf and the shelf sides even. Then glue and secure each shelf side to the top shelf, using two screws driven through the pilot holes in the top shelf and into the middle of the shelf side's edge.

7. Make sure that the shelf sides are parallel; then measure between the sides for the width of the upper and lower back panels (approximately 13½″). Cut two back panels from ½ × 5½ pine lattice.

8. Using the same measurement, cut the bottom shelf from ½ × 3½ pine lattice.

9. Draw a line 1⁄16″ from and parallel with one long edge (bottom) of the lower back panel. Locate and mark the middle of the line. On the line, mark 2⁵⁄16″ twice at either side of the central mark. Using the ²³⁄64″ bit, drill ¼″-deep peg holes for the Shaker pegs at each mark. (See the note in the Materials list.)

10. Apply glue to the edges of the upper back panel, and position the panel so that it is flush with the back edges of the top shelf and shelf sides. Secure the panel with brads driven through the pilot

holes in the top shelf and in the shelf sides.

11. Apply glue to the short edges of the bottom shelf, and position the shelf so that its back edge is flush with the back edges of the upper back panel and the shelf sides. Secure the shelf with brads nailed through the pilot holes in the shelf sides.

12. On each shelf side, mark for another pilot hole ½″ from the front edge and centered on the edge of the bottom shelf. Using the No. 61 bit, drill pilot holes through the shelf sides, into the edge of the bottom shelf, and secure with brads.

13. Apply glue to the top and side edges of the lower back panel, and position the panel so that it is flush with the back edge of the bottom shelf and the shelf sides. Secure the panel with brads driven through the pilot holes in the shelf sides.

14. Glue the Shaker pegs into the peg holes.

15. Paint the assembly medium-grey-blue.

16. Apply the satin finish.

17. Nail the sawtooth hangers to the back of the top shelf, spacing them ½″ from the sides and flush with the top edge.

11. Farm-Scene Knickknacks

MATERIALS

- 16" length of ¼ × ⅞ clear pine lattice
- 20" length of ½ × 5½ clear pine lattice
- Drill bits: No. 61 (wire gauge) and ⁵⁄₆₄"
- Four #19 × ½" wire brads
- Small amount of black, white, and pink synthetic suede
- One ¼ × ¼ × ¼" copper bell
- 1" length of thread-covered floral wire
- One round toothpick
- 1⅛ × 5" rectangle of white decorative adhesive covering
- Acrylic paints: light apricot (LA), bright red (BR), white (W), ultramarine (U), black (B), dark pink (DP), dark yellow (DY), medium-yellow-brown (MYB), light pink (LP), light red-brown (LRB), medium-yellow-green, and medium-grey
- High-gloss finish

Farm-Scene Knickknacks

The Farmer and His Animals*

1. Cut one farmer (11–1) and one each of his animals from ½ × 5½ pine lattice. There are animal-body patterns for the following: a horse (11–3), cow (11–8), sheep (11–9), pig (11–11), dog (11–13), duck (11–16), rooster (11–18), and rabbit (11–19).

2. Use the ⁵⁄₆₄" bit to drill ¼"-deep tail holes, where indicated by the small arrows on the horse (11–3), cow (11–8), and pig (11–11).

3. To paint the pieces, refer to the Materials list for the paint color codes. Extend all colors onto the edge surfaces, except where otherwise indicated. For additional painting directions, see the instructions for the individual pieces.

---

*Refer to the General Directions for the techniques needed to complete this project.

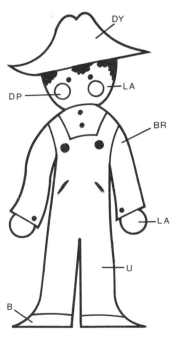

11–1. Farmer (cut one).

11–2. Back view of the farmer.

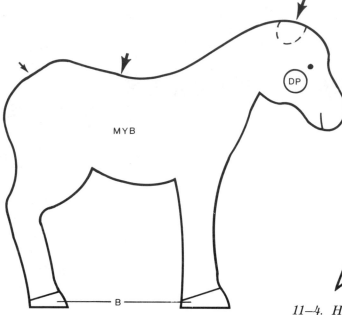

MYB

B

11–3. Horse (cut one).

11–4. Horse's forelock (cut one).

11–5. Horse's mane (cut one).

11–6. Horse's, sheep's, and pig's ears (cut two for each). Also, cow's tail tassel (cut one).

11–7. Horse's tail (cut one).

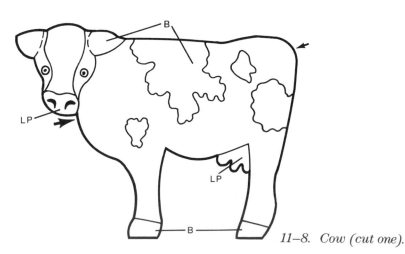

B

LP

LP

B

11–8. Cow (cut one).

4. Apply the high-gloss finish after painting and before using tacky glue to adhere such parts as the ears, tails, mane, and forelock.

Farmer

1. Paint the back of the farmer as shown on 11–2, repeating the colors used for the front.

2. Paint the eyes and hair black. Use black to paint the buttons and pockets of the overalls. Paint the shirt buttons white.

Horse

1. Paint the eyes and mouth black, extending the mouth across the front of the face. For the nose, paint a $\frac{3}{16}$″-wide × $\frac{1}{8}$″-high oval on the front of the face, where indicated by the dot on 11–3.

2. Cut one forelock (11–4), one mane (11–5), two ears (11–6), and one tail (11–7) from black synthetic suede.

3. Glue the rounded end of the forelock to the middle of the edge surface where indicated by the large arrow closest to the face on 11–3.

4. Glue the straight edge of the mane to the middle of the edge surface, between the large arrows on 11–3. Have the fringed edge of the mane facing the left side of the horse.

5. Glue the ears to the sides of the head where indicated by the dashed line on 11–3.

6. Glue the end of the tail into the tail hole.

Cow

1. Use the No. 61 bit to drill a $\frac{1}{4}$″-deep pilot hole for the bell where indicated by the large arrow on 11–8.

2. Paint both sides of the cow in the same manner, with the exception of the face. Don't extend the face onto the edge surface, and omit it from the back of the cow's head. Do extend the ears onto the edge surface and paint the edges of the ears on the back of the cow, as shown by the dashed lines on 11–8.

3. Paint the eyes white. Use black to paint the pupils and nostrils.

4. Insert a brad through the bell's loop. Then insert the brad into the pilot hole, and use the tip of a small screwdriver to push the brad into the hole until $\frac{1}{4}$″ of the brad extends from the pilot hole and the bell swings freely.

5. Cut a $\frac{1}{8}$″ × $1\frac{3}{8}$″ strip of white synthetic suede for the tail.

6. Cut one tail tassel (11–6) from black synthetic suede.

7. Glue the rounded end of the tail tassel to the end of the tail. Glue the end of the tail into the tail hole. Referring to the photograph, adhere the tail tassel to the left back leg.

Sheep

1. Paint the body white and allow to dry. Use a 1 × 1″ sponge to dab a thick coat of white paint on the sides of the sheep to create dense, raised areas.

2. Paint the eyes white and the pupils black.

3. Cut two ears (11–6) and one tail (11–10) from black synthetic suede.

4. With the pointed tips of the ears touching, glue the ears to the top surface of the head where indicated by the large arrow on 11–9.

5. Adhere the tip of the tail to the back of the sheep, where indicated by the small arrow on 11–9.

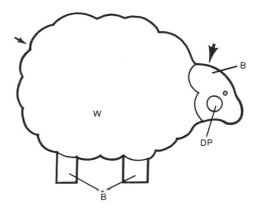

11–9. Sheep (cut one).

11–10. Sheep's tail (cut one).

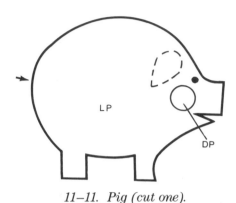

11–11. Pig (cut one).

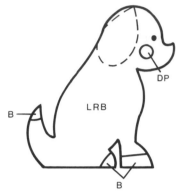

11–13. Dog (cut one).

11–12. Front view of the pig's face.

11–14. Front view of the dog's face.

11–15. Dog's ear (cut two).

Pig

1. Paint the eyes black. Use black to paint the nostrils on the front of the face, as shown on 11–12.

2. Cut two ears (11–6) from pink synthetic suede.

3. Glue the ears to the sides of the head where indicated by the dashed line on 11–11.

4. Coil the floral wire loosely around the toothpick. Glue one end of the wire into the tail hole.

Dog

1. Paint the eyes black. Use black to paint the nose and mouth on the front of the face, as shown on 11–14.

2. Cut two ears (11–15) from black synthetic suede.

3. Glue the ears to the sides of the head where indicated by the dashed line on 11–13.

Duck

1. Paint the eyes black.

2. Cut two wings (11–17) from white synthetic suede.

3. Glue the wings to the sides of the body where indicated by the dashed line on 11–16.

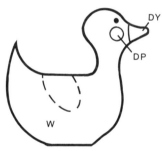

11–16. Duck (cut one).

11–17. Duck's wing (cut two).

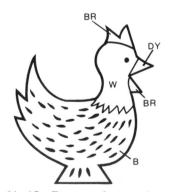

11–18. Rooster (cut one).

Rooster

1. Paint the eyes black.

2. Paint white feathers on top of the black area in 11–18, continuing them onto the edge surfaces.

Rabbit

1. Paint the eyes and whiskers black and the nose light pink, as shown on 11–20.

11–19. Rabbit (cut one).

11–20. Front view of the rabbit's face.

Barn

1. Cut a 6⅝″ length of ¼ × ⅞ pine lattice for the base.

2. Cut one barn (11–21) from ½ × 5½ pine lattice.

3. Glue the base, centered, over the bottom of the barn. Secure with three evenly spaced brads.

4. Cut two 2½″ lengths of ¼ × ⅞ pine lattice for the roof gable.

5. Cut one 3⅞″ length of ¼ × ⅞ pine lattice for the roof eaves. To indicate the eave angles, measure 1¾″ from the right end of the piece and draw a line across the width. Turn the piece over, measure 1¾″ from the left end, and draw a line across the width. Cut the eave angles by sawing from one line to the other.

6. Butt the gable pieces at the barn's peak. Sand the butted end of each piece to a slight angle, until they fit tightly together.

7. With their long edges flush with the back of the barn, glue the gable pieces to the barn peak.

8. Glue the eave pieces, with their eave angles facing up, under the gable pieces and flush with the back of the barn.

9. Paint the barn bright red, the base medium-yellow-green, and the roof medium-grey.

10. Apply the high-gloss finish.

11. Cut six ⅛ × 5″ strips of white decorative adhesive covering for the barn door.

12. Adhere the strips to the barn, where indicated on 11–21, mitring the corners with a craft knife.

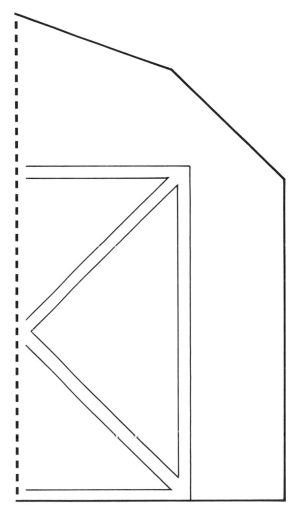

11–21. Half-pattern for the barn (cut one).

12. Welcome Sign

Welcome Sign

MATERIALS

- 7 × 10″ rectangle of ¼″ birch plywood
- Drill bit: ⅛″
- 23″ length of ⅛″-wide green grosgrain ribbon
- Acrylic paints: dark pink, dark green, white, dark yellow, and medium-grey-blue
- High-gloss finish

Welcome Sign*

1. Cut one welcome sign (12–1) from ¼″ plywood.

2. Transfer the lettering (12–2) onto the sign, using the dashed lines as a guide.

3. Using the ⅛″ bit, drill holes through the sign where indicated by the stars on 12–1.

4. Paint the heart dark pink, the leaves and stems dark green, and the flower petals white. Use dark yellow to paint the flower centers. Paint the lettering medium-grey-blue.

5. Apply the high-gloss finish.

6. Insert the ribbon ends into the holes from the front of the sign. With the ribbon ends even, draw the ribbon through the holes, leaving a 1¾″-long loop at the front. Tie a double-knot onto the loop and make a bow. Trim the ribbon ends at an angle.

---

*Refer to the General Directions for the techniques needed to complete this project.

12–1. Half-pattern for the welcome sign (cut one).

12–2. Lettering for the welcome sign.

13. Checkered Step Stool

Checkered Step Stool

Checkered Step Stool*

1. Cut a 21¼″ length of 1 × 10 pine for the top.

2. Cut two sides (13–1) from 1 × 10 pine.

3. Cut one brace (13–2) from 1 × 8 pine.

4. Draw two lines 2⅜″ from and parallel with each short side of the top. Measuring from one long edge, mark the following three points on each line: 1″, 4⅝″, and 8¼″. Draw another line down the middle of the length. Measuring from one short edge, mark the following points on the line: 3¾″, 8¼″, 13″, and 17½″.

5. Using the ¹⁄₁₆″ bit, drill pilot holes through the top at each mark and through each side, where indicated by the stars on 13–1.

6. Glue the sides (13–1) to the brace (13–2), centering the pilot holes in the sides over the side edges of the brace. Secure with three screws driven through the pilot holes in each side.

7. Glue the top to the sides and brace, centering the pilot holes in the top over the edges of the sides and brace. Secure with 10 screws driven through the top.

8. Locate the middle of the top. Working from the middle out, mark a grid of 6 squares × 14 squares, with each square measuring 1½″. (There will be

---

*Refer to the General Directions for the techniques needed to complete this project.

62

MATERIALS

- 18″ length of 1 × 8 clear pine
- 43″ length of 1 × 10 clear pine
- Drill bit: ¹⁄₁₆″
- Sixteen #6 × 1½″ flat-head wood screws
- One roll each of 1″- and 2″-wide masking tape
- Acrylic paints: ecru, black, and terra cotta
- High-gloss and satin finishes

approximately ⅛″ remaining on all sides for the terra-cotta border described in step 11.) Cut 2″-wide masking tape into forty-two 1½″ squares. Starting at the lower-right square on a long side of the top, cover every other square of the grid with a square of tape. Frame the grid with strips of 1″-wide masking tape, butted to all sides of the grid.

9. Paint the untaped squares of the grid ecru; allow them to dry, and then remove the tape squares.

10. Now cover the ecru squares with the squares of tape. Paint the untaped squares of the grid black, allow them to dry, and then remove the tape.

11. To mask for the ⅛″-wide terra-cotta border around the grid, cover over each side of the grid with a strip of 1″-wide masking tape, butted to the edge of the grid.

12. Use terra cotta to paint the border around the grid and the rest of the assembly.

13. To mask for the black stripe around the side edges of the top, measure ³⁄₁₆″ down from the top edge and ³⁄₁₆″ up from the bottom edge and draw guidelines around all four sides. Butt 1″-wide masking tape to the top and bottom guidelines. Paint the stripe black, allow it to dry, and then remove the tape.

14. Apply the high-gloss finish to the top and its side edges.

15. Apply the satin finish to the rest of the assembly.

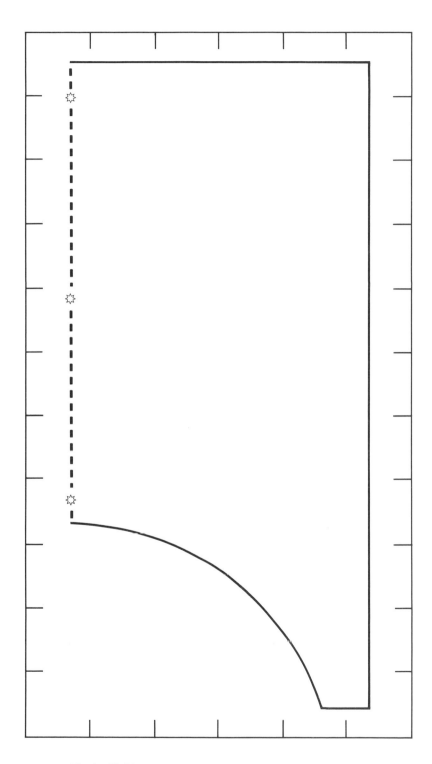

13–1. *Half-pattern for the stool's side. Each square equals 1". Enlarge and cut two.*

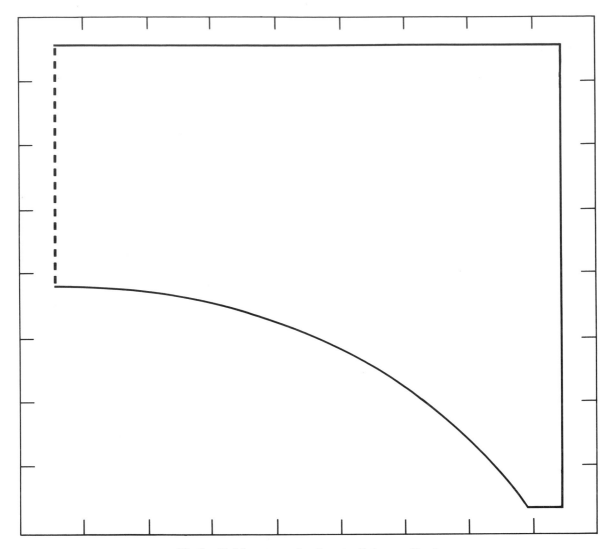

13–2. Half-pattern for the stool's brace. Each square equals 1". Enlarge and cut one.

14. Sunflower Plant Stick

MATERIALS

- 6″ length of ¼ × 5¼ clear pine lattice
- 14¼″ length of ⁵⁄₁₆″ dowelling
- 10 white, 10-mm, regular-hole, round wood beads
- Drill bit: No. 61 (wire gauge)
- Two #19 × ½″ wire brads
- Acrylic paints: dark yellow, very dark red-brown, dark red-brown, light yellow-green, and light red-brown
- Acrylic metallic paint: bronze
- High-gloss finish

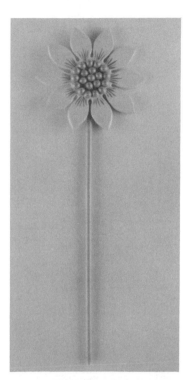

Sunflower Plant Stick*

1. Cut one sunflower (14–1) from ¼ × 5¼ pine lattice.

2. Mark 2⅛″ from one end (top) of the dowelling. Whittle a ⁵⁄₁₆″-wide, flat gluing area from the mark to the top. Whittle the bottom end to a point.

3. Mark ¼″ and ⅝″ from the top end of the dowelling for two pilot holes. Using the No. 61 bit, drill pilot holes through the dowelling.

4. Paint the sunflower dark yellow. On the back of the sunflower only, leave the area that is indicated by the dashed line on the drawing unpainted.

5. On the front of the sunflower only, paint the circle on the drawing very dark red-brown and the petal details dark red-brown.

6. Paint the dowelling light yellow-green, leaving the upper 1″ of the whittled area unpainted.

7. Apply glue to the unpainted area of the

---

*Refer to the General Directions for the techniques needed to complete this project. Materials and directions are for one plant stick.

Sunflower Plant Stick. Top: *entire stick.* Bottom: *closeup of flower.*

dowelling, position it over the unpainted area on the back of the sunflower, and secure with the two brads.

8. Split the ten 10-mm beads in half for the seeds.

9. Paint the seeds light red-brown. Use bronze metallic to paint a ⅛″-diameter dot at the middle top of each seed.

10. Use tacky glue to adhere one seed to the middle of the circle. For the second row, adhere six seeds around the middle seed. (Position the seeds so that their half-holes cover the tips of the brads.) Adhere the 13 remaining seeds around the second row.

11. Apply the high-gloss finish.

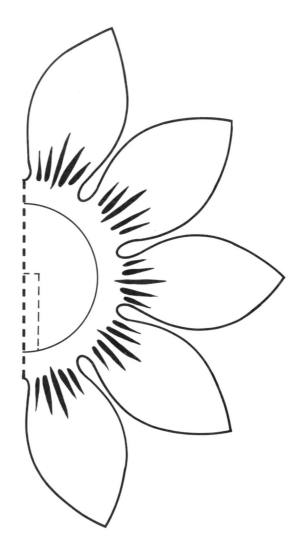

14–1. Half-pattern for the sunflower (cut one).

15. Monarch-Butterfly Plant Stick

MATERIALS

- 5½ × 3″ rectangle of ¼″ birch plywood
- 15″ length of ³⁄₁₆″ dowelling
- Drill bit: ¹⁄₁₆″
- Long-nose pliers
- 3½″ length of #18-gauge floral wire
- Acrylic paints: black (B), medium-orange (MO), medium-yellow (MY), and medium-red-brown (MRB)
- High-gloss finish

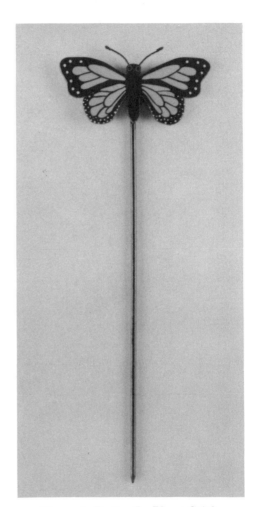

Monarch-Butterfly Plant Stick

Monarch-Butterfly Plant Stick*

1. Cut one butterfly (15–1) from ¼″ plywood.

2. Using the ¹⁄₁₆″-bit, drill ³⁄₁₆″-deep antennae holes where indicated by the arrow on 15–1.

3. Mark 1¼″ from one end (top) of the dowelling. Whittle a ³⁄₁₆″-wide, flat gluing area from the mark to the top. Whittle the bottom end to a point.

4. Cut the length of floral wire in half for the antennae. Using the long-nose pliers, bend one end of each antenna into a ³⁄₁₆″-long, flattened loop. With the loops facing the tips of the wings, use tacky glue to adhere the other ends into the antennae holes. Curve the antennae, as shown in the photograph.

5. Glue the flat end of the dowelling to the back of the butterfly where indicated by the dashed line in the drawing.

6. Use black to paint the back of the butterfly, the antennae, and the dowelling.

7. Paint the front of the butterfly by referring to the Materials list for the color codes.

8. Apply the high-gloss finish.

---

*Refer to the General Directions for the techniques needed to complete this project.

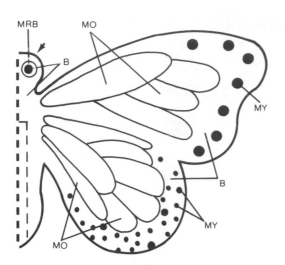

15–1. *Half-pattern for the monarch butterfly (cut one).*

15–2. *Closeup of butterfly.*

16. Sheep Plant Stand

MATERIALS

- 14 × 22″ rectangle of ¼″ birch plywood
- 10″ length of ¼ × 5¼ clear pine lattice
- 7″ length of ½ × 5½ clear pine lattice
- 50″ length of 1 × 8 clear pine
- One 1¹⁄₁₆″-long × ⁷⁄₃₂″-diameter wooden axle peg
- Two white, 12-mm, regular-hole, round wood beads
- Drill bit: No. 61 (wire gauge), ¹⁄₁₆″, and ⁷⁄₃₂″
- Five #6 × 1½″ flat-head wood screws
- Two #19 × ½″ wire brads
- Twenty-eight #18 × ⅞″ wire brads
- One ½″-long × ¼″-diameter screw eye
- Two adjustable pliers
- One 1¼ × 1 × 1¼″ copper bell
- 1″-wide brush, with coarse bristles
- Acrylic paints: white, black, dark red-brown, and pale blue-grey
- Acrylic gesso
- High-gloss and satin finishes

Sheep Plant Stand

Sheep Plant Stand*

1. Cut a 7⅛ × 15″ rectangle from 1 × 8 pine for the shelf.

2. Cut one head (16–1) from 1 × 8 pine. Transfer the outline of the tinted (gluing) area onto the sides of the head.

3. Cut one front and one back (16–2) from 1 × 8 pine. (Omit the notch on the pattern from the back piece.)

4. Cut two sides (16–3) from ¼″ plywood.

5. Cut four hooves (16–4) from ½ × 5½ pine lattice.

6. Cut two ears (16–5) and one tail (16–6) from ¼ × 5¼ pine lattice. The pattern for the ear (16–6) shows the orientation of the right ear; the left ear is a mirror image.

*Refer to the General Directions for the techniques needed to complete this project.

7. Mark the middle of the edge surface of one short side of the shelf. (This is now the back of the shelf.) Using the ⁷⁄₃₂″ bit, drill a ¾″-deep axle-peg hole to be used for attaching the tail (16–6). (The axle-peg shank will extend ¹⁄₁₆″ from the hole after assembly with the tail.)

8. Using the ⁷⁄₃₂″ bit, drill a hole through the tail (16–6), where indicated by the star on the pattern.

9. Mark for a pilot hole 3¼″ from the front of the shelf and centered from side to side.

10. Draw two lines 2¾″ from and parallel with the back and front of the shelf. Mark two points on each line, ¾″ from each long side.

11. Using the ¹⁄₁₆″ bit, drill pilot holes through the shelf at each mark.

12. Using the No. 61 bit, drill a ⅛″-deep pilot hole into the neck, where indicated by the large arrow on 16–1.

16–1. Sheep's head. Each square equals 1". Enlarge and cut one.

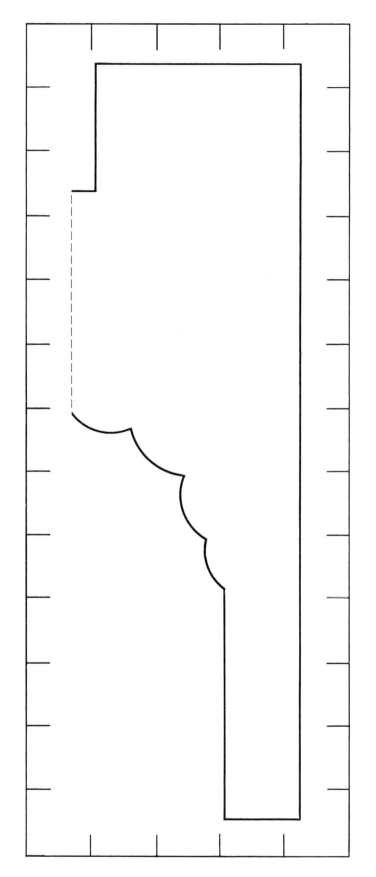

16–2. Half-pattern for the sheep, front and back. Each square equals 1". Enlarge and cut two.

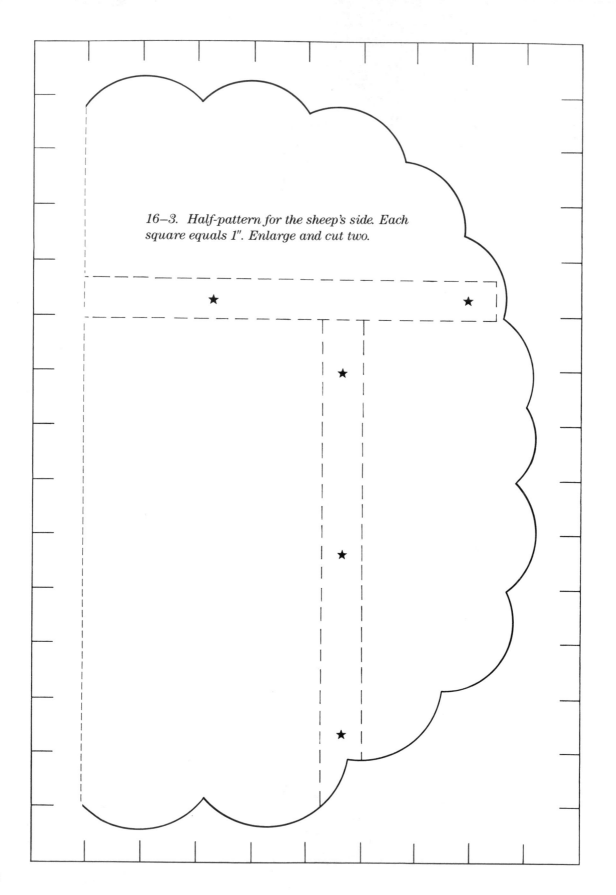

16–3. *Half-pattern for the sheep's side. Each square equals 1". Enlarge and cut two.*

13. Using the No. 61 bit, drill pilot holes through the sides (16–3), hooves (16–4), and ears (16–5), where indicated by the stars on the patterns.

14. Apply glue to the notch edges of the head (16–1). Slip the middle front of the shelf into the notch. Secure with one screw driven through the pilot hole located 3¼″ from the front of the shelf and into the edge surface of the notch.

15. Apply glue to the notch edges and top edges of the front piece (16–2). Position the notch around the sheep's neck, and center its top edge under the two pilot holes in the front of the shelf. Secure with two screws driven through the shelf. Glue the back piece (16–2) to the underside of the shelf, centering its top edge on the two pilot holes in the back of the shelf, and secure with two screws driven through the shelf.

16. Glue the sides (16–3) to the side edges of both the front and back and the shelf, where indicated by the dashed line on 16–3. Secure each side with ten #18 × ⅞″ brads nailed through the pilot holes in the hooves.

17. Glue the hooves (16–4) to the bottoms of the legs of the front and back pieces (16–2), where indicated by the dashed line on 16–4. Secure each with two #18 × ⅞″ brads nailed through the pilot holes in the hooves.

18. To create the angle on the underside of each ear (16–5), whittle a flat surface from the dashed line to the dot so that the thickness at the dot is ⅛″.

19. Split the 12-mm beads in half for the eyes and nose. (Discard one-half.) With the half-holes angled, as shown by the dashed line on 16–1, glue the eyes to the sides of the head, where indicated by the dots on the pattern. With the half-holes held vertically, glue the nose to the front surface of the head, where indicated by the small arrow on 16–1. Fill the half-holes with paste wood filler, allow to dry, and sand smooth.

20. Use white to paint the head (paint ¹⁄₁₆″ into the gluing outlines), shelf, sides, and upper portions of the front and back. Paint all edges and the underside of the assembly. Paint the axle-peg cap and all sides of the tail white.

21. Working from the outside edges towards the middle, use gesso and the 1″-wide brush to paint

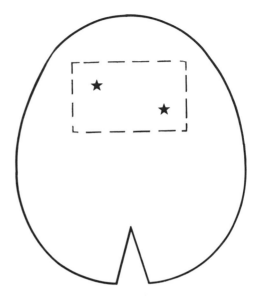

16–4. Sheep's hoof (cut four).

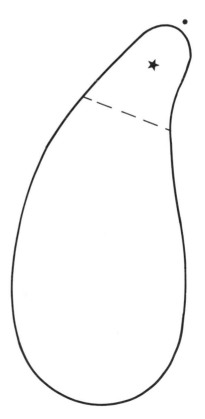

16–5. Sheep's ear (cut two).

overlapping circles to simulate fleece. Paint 2″-diameter circles on the shelf and the sides. Paint 1″-diameter circles on the head and the front and back. Paint 1″-diameter circles on one face surface of the tail, working from the top of the tail towards the bottom.

22. Use black to paint the face, lower legs, and hooves.

23. Paint the ears (16–5) black, omitting the whittled areas on the backs.

24. Use black to paint a ⅛″-diameter circle in the middle of each eye for the pupil. Around the pupils, paint a ⅛″ band of dark red-brown. Paint the base of the eyes black.

25. Glue the whittled surface of the ears (16–5) to the sides of the head, where indicated by the gluing outline on 16–1. Secure each with one #19 × ½″ brad nailed through the pilot hole in the ear.

26. Referring to the photograph, use a 1 × 1″ sponge to sponge pale blue-grey highlights as follows: a ⅜″-wide band over the white areas of the sides of the head and neck, a ⅜″-wide band along the scalloped edges between the feet on the front and back, a ⅜″-wide border around the gessoed surface of the tail, and a ¾″-wide border around the sides of the body.

27. Apply the high-gloss finish to the eyes and nose.

28. Apply the satin finish to the rest of the assembly, the tail, and the axle-peg cap.

29. Apply a small amount of glue into the peg hole in the rear of the shelf. Insert the axle peg into the hole in the tail (16–6) and then into the peg hole in the shelf. (Have the gessoed surface of the tail facing out.) The tail should swing freely.

30. Use the two adjustable pliers to slightly pry open the screw eye. Hook the bell onto the screw eye, and close the screw eye with the pliers. Thread the screw eye–bell assembly into the pilot hole in the neck. Have the short side of the bell parallel with the body.

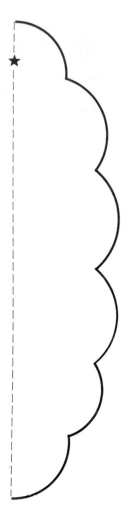

16–6. Half-pattern for the sheep's tail (cut one).

17. Checkerboard Serving Tray and Heart Checkers

MATERIALS

- 71″ length of ¼ × 1⅜ clear pine lattice
- 9″ length of ¼ × 5¼ clear pine lattice
- 23″ length of 1 × 12 clear pine
- Drill bit: No. 61 (wire gauge)
- Twenty-eight #18 × ⅞″ wire brads
- One roll each of 1″- and 2″-wide masking tape
- Acrylic paints: medium-blue-grey, black, bright red, and ecru
- High-gloss and satin finishes

Checkerboard Serving Tray and Heart Checkers

Checkerboard Serving Tray*

1. Use the 23″ length of 1 × 8 pine for the tray.

2. Cut two lengths of ¼ × 1⅜ pine lattice to the length of the tray's short sides (approximately 11¼″). Cut two 23½″ lengths of ¼ × 1⅜ pine lattice to complete the frame.

3. Draw a line down the length of each frame piece, ½″ from and parallel with a long edge. (This is now the bottom of each frame piece.) On each short piece, measure from one end and mark the following points on the line: ½″, 3⅟₁₆″, 5⅝″, 8⅛″, and 10¾″. On each long piece, measure from one end and mark the following points: ½″, 3⁷⁄₁₆″, 6⅛″, 9⅟₁₆″, 11¾″, 14¹³⁄₁₆″, 17⅜″, 20⁵⁄₁₆″, and 23″.

4. Using the No. 61 bit, drill pilot holes through the frame pieces at each mark.

5. Locate the middle of the tray. Working from the middle out, mark a grid of 8 squares × 8 squares, with each square measuring 1⅜″. (There will be approximately ⅛″ remaining on both long sides for the border described in step 7.)

*Refer to the General Directions for the techniques needed to complete this project.

6. Cut 2″-wide masking tape into thirty-two 1⅜″ squares. Starting at the lower-left square on a long side of the board, cover every other square of the grid with a square of tape. Frame the grid with strips of 1″-wide masking tape, butted to all sides of the grid.

7. Paint the untaped squares of the grid medium-grey-blue, allow them to dry, and then remove the tape.

8. To mask for the ⅛″-wide black border around the grid, cover over each side of the grid with a strip of 1″-wide masking tape, butted to the edge of the grid. On both short sides of the tray, adhere strips of tape spaced ⅛″ from the grid. The ⅛″ space on both long sides of the tray completes the border.

9. Paint the border black, allow it to dry, and then remove the tape.

10. As shown in the photograph, transfer the heart motif (17–1) to each end of the tray, butting it to the border and centering it from left to right.

11. Paint the backgrounds medium-grey-blue, the middle hearts bright red, and the remainder of the motifs ecru.

12. Glue the two short frame pieces to the ends of the tray. Center the pilot holes over the edge of the tray, and allow the frame to extend ⅛″ below the bottom of the tray. Secure each with five brads nailed through the pilot holes. Glue the long frame pieces to the sides of the tray and, at the same time, to the ends of the short frame pieces. Secure each with nine brads nailed through the pilot holes.

13. Paint the frame and the bottom of the assembly black.

14. Apply the high-gloss finish.

Heart Checkers

1. Cut twenty-four heart checkers (17–2) from ¼ × 5¼ pine lattice.

2. Paint twelve checkers black and twelve bright red.

3. Apply the satin finish.

17–2. Heart checker (cut 24).

17–1. Half-pattern for the heart motif.

18. Country-Heart Coasters and Caddy

MATERIALS

- 24 × 24″ square of ¼″ birch plywood
- 14″ length of ½ × 5½ clear pine lattice
- 12″ length of ⁷⁄₁₆″ dowelling
- Drill bit: ²⁷⁄₆₄″
- Acrylic paints: bright red, medium-blue-grey, and black
- High-gloss waterproof finish

Country-Heart Coasters and Caddy

Country-Heart Coasters*

1. Cut eight coasters (18–1) from ¼″ plywood.

2. Paint the coasters bright red.

3. Apply the high-gloss waterproof finish.

Caddy

1. Cut two caddy sides (18–2) from ½ × 5½ pine lattice.

2. Cut four 2½″ lengths of dowelling.

3. Using the ²⁷⁄₆₄″ bit, drill ¼″-deep holes where indicated by the stars on 18–2.

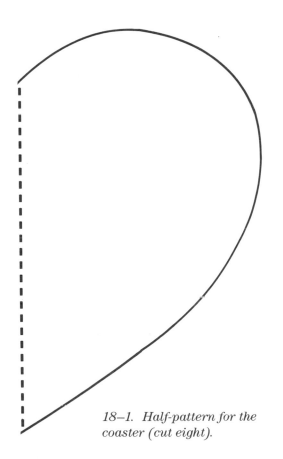

18–1. Half-pattern for the coaster (cut eight).

---

*Refer to the General Directions for the techniques needed to complete this project.

77

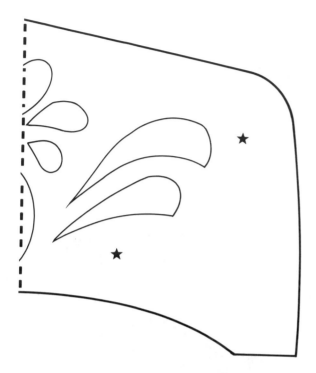

18–2. Half-pattern for the caddy's side (cut two).

4. Glue the lengths of dowelling into the holes in one caddy side and then into the corresponding holes in the other.

5. Paint the assembly medium-blue-grey.

6. Use black to paint the heart motif on each caddy side.

7. Apply the high-gloss waterproof finish.

19. Vegetable Ornaments and Garden Rake Display Rack

MATERIALS

- 33″ length of ¼ × 5¼ clear pine lattice
- 12″ length of 1 × 3 clear pine
- 20″ length of ⁵⁄₁₆″ dowelling
- 24″ length of ½″ dowelling
- Eight white, 10-mm, regular-hole, round wood beads
- Four white, 12-mm, regular-hole, round wood beads
- Drill bits: ⅛″ and ⁵⁄₁₆″
- Spade bit: ½″
- Five ½″-long × ¼″-diameter screw eyes
- Two 2½″-long sawtooth hangers, with supplied brads
- 45″ length of plastic raffia
- 41″ length of ⅛″-diameter round caning
- Acrylic paints: medium-orange, light yellow-green, medium-olive-green, black, dark orange-red, medium-yellow-green, dark yellow, and light grey-green
- Wood stain: dark walnut
- High-gloss and satin finishes

Vegetable Ornaments*

1. Cut one each of the following patterns from ¼ × 5¼ pine lattice: carrot (19–1), carrot-top detail (19–2), tomato (19–3), tomato calyx (19–4), corn-husk base (19–6), left corn husk (19–7), right corn husk (19–8), celery stalks (19–9), and celery top (19–10). Cut two pea pods (19–5) from ¼ × 5¼ pine lattice.

2. See the sections that follow for assembling and painting the individual pieces. Remember to extend

---

*Refer to the General Directions for the techniques needed to complete this project.

Vegetable Ornaments and Garden Rake Display Rack. Top: *entire rack.* Bottom: *closeup of vegetables.*

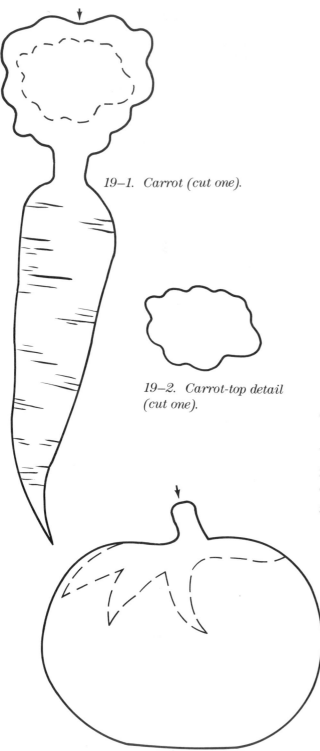

19–1. Carrot (cut one).

19–2. Carrot-top detail (cut one).

all colors onto the edge surfaces and the backs of the ornaments.

3. Apply the high-gloss finish after painting.

4. Use an ice pick to make ⅛″-deep pilot holes for the screw eyes, where indicated by the arrows on the patterns. Thread the screw eyes into the pilot holes. Make sure that the screw-eye holes are at right angles to the fronts of the ornaments, as shown in the photograph.

5. Cut raffia to the length specified for each ornament. Insert the raffia through the screw eyes, and knot ¾″ from the ends. Trim the ends close to the knots.

Carrot

1. Glue the carrot-top detail (19–2) to the top of the carrot where indicated by the dashed line on 19–1.

2. Paint the carrot medium-orange and the carrot top light yellow-green. Sponge medium-olive-green paint on the carrot top, using a 1 × 1″ sponge. Paint the carrot details black.

3. Cut a 6½″ length of raffia.

Tomato

1. Glue the tomato calyx (19–4) to the tomato where indicated by the dashed line on 19–3.

2. Paint the tomato dark orange-red and the tomato calyx and stem medium-yellow-green.

3. Cut a 5½″ length of raffia.

19–3. Tomato (cut one).

19–4. Tomato calyx (cut one).

Peas

1. Glue one pea pod on top of the other, where indicated by the dashed line on 19–5.

2. Split three 10-mm beads and three 12-mm beads in half for the peas. With the half-holes held vertical, glue the peas to the top pea pod, where indicated by the dots on 19–5. Starting at the bottom of the pod, glue the peas in the following order: one 10 mm, three 12 mm, and two 10 mm.

3. For the bottom pea pod, trim ⅛″ off one side of a 12-mm half-bead and split a 10-mm half-bead in half again (discard the remainder). Glue the peas to the bottom pea pod. Starting at the bottom of the pod, glue in this order: one 10 mm, two 12 mm, the trimmed 12-mm half-bead (butt the trimmed edge to the left side of the top pea pod), and the 10-mm quarter-bead (butt the cut edge to the left side of the top pea pod).

4. Paint the assembly light yellow-green.

5. Make the pilot hole for the screw eye in the bottom pea pod.

6. Cut a 9″ length of raffia.

Corn

1. Transfer the outline of the tinted (kernel) area on 19–6 to the corn-husk base.

2. Glue the left (19–7) and right (19–8) corn husks to the base where indicated by the dashed lines on 19–6.

3. Split five 10-mm beads and one 12-mm bead in half for the kernels. Split two 10-mm half-beads in half again to make four quarter-beads.

4. With the half- and quarter-holes held vertical, test-fit the kernels, where indicated by the dots on 19–6. Starting at the bottom, position the left row in the following order (trimming to fit as necessary): two 12 mm, three 10 mm quarter-beads (butt their cut edges to the side of the right corn husk), and four 10-mm half-beads. Starting at the bottom, position the second row: one 10-mm quarter-bead (butt the cut edge to the side of the right corn husk) and three 10 mm.

5. Paint the corn husks light yellow-green. Use dark yellow to paint the kernel area of the base and the kernels.

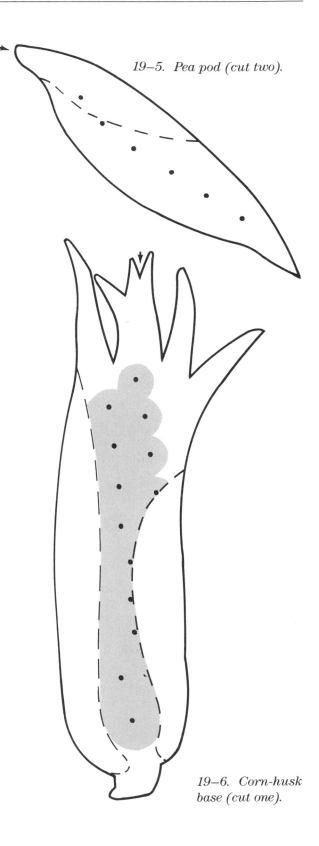

19–5. Pea pod (cut two).

19–6. Corn-husk base (cut one).

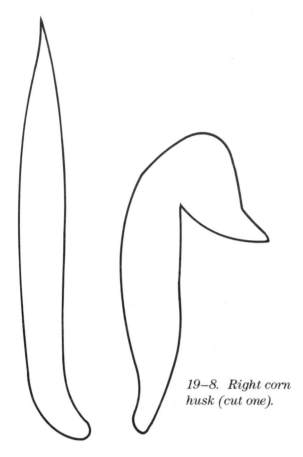

19–8. Right corn husk (cut one).

19–7. Left corn husk (cut one).

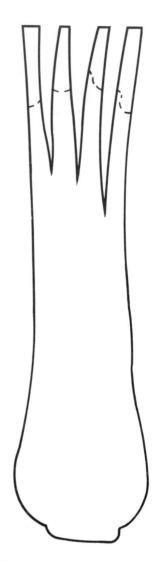

19–9. Celery stalks (cut one).

6. Use tacky glue to adhere the kernels to the corn-husk base.

7. Cut a 6½″ length of raffia.

Celery
1. Glue the celery top (19–10) to the celery stalks where indicated by the dashed lines on 19–9.

2. Paint the assembly light yellow-green.

3. Paint the celery stalks with the dry-brush technique. Dip the brush into medium-olive-green, and wipe it on paper towels to remove excess paint. Using long strokes, brush down the length of the stalks, allowing some light yellow-green to show through. Allow the paint to dry. Repeat using light grey-green, allowing some of the light yellow-green and medium-olive-green to show through.

4. Using a 1 × 1″ sponge, sponge medium-olive-green paint on the celery tops in an irregular pattern. Allow the paint to dry, and then sponge on highlights in light grey-green.

5. Cut a 5½″ length of raffia.

Garden Rake Display Rack
1. Cut one rake head (19–11) from 1 × 3 pine.

2. Cut seven 2½″ lengths of ⁵⁄₁₆″ dowelling for the tines.

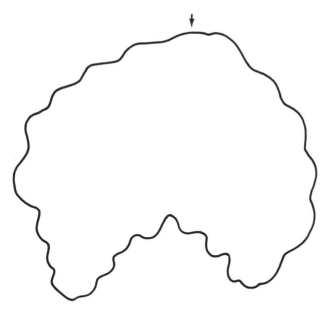

19–10. Celery top (cut one).

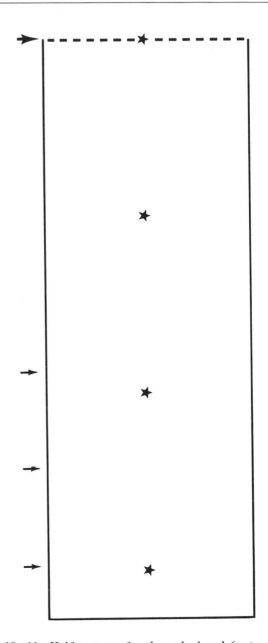

3. Cut caning into 10½″, 13½″, and 17″ lengths. (Soak in warm water for 2 hours, or until pliable, before assembly.)

4. Use the 24″ length of ½″ dowelling for the handle. Measure 4″, 5⅛″, and 6¼″ from one end (top) of the handle. Using the ⅛″ bit, drill holes for the braces through the handle.

5. Using the ⅛″ bit, drill ¼″-deep holes for the braces, centered on the edge surface, where indicated by the small arrows on 19–11.

6. Using the ⁵⁄₁₆″ bit, drill ½″-deep holes for the tines, where indicated by the stars on 19–11.

7. Using the ½″ spade bit, drill a ¾″-deep hole for the handle, centered on the edge surface, where indicated by the large arrow on 19–11.

8. Glue the top of the handle into the handle hole in the rake head. Make sure that the brace holes in the handle are parallel with the rake head.

9. Glue the tines into the tine holes.

10. Insert the caning through the brace holes in the handle. Insert the shortest piece through the hole closest to the rake head, the next longest through the middle hole, and the longest through the remaining hole. Referring to the photograph, glue the caning ends into the brace holes in the rake head.

19–11. Half-pattern for the rake head (cut one).

Allow the caning to dry overnight before staining.

11. Apply the dark walnut stain with a brush, wiping off the excess with a soft cloth.

12. Apply the satin finish.

13. Nail the sawtooth hangers to the back of the rake head, spacing them ½″ from the top edge and sides.

20. Cow Wind Chimes

MATERIALS
• 12″ length of ¼ × 5¼ clear pine lattice • 6″ length of ½ × 5½ clear pine lattice • Drill bit: 1⁄16″ • Fifteen ½″-long × ¼″-diameter screw eyes • Two adjustable pliers • Needle-nose pliers • 6¾″ length of white, worsted-weight, cotton yarn • 18″ length of #16-gauge copper wire • Three ¼ × ¼ × ¼″ small copper bells • Three 1 × ¾ × 1″ medium copper bells • Four 1¼ × 1 × 1¼″ large copper bells • ⅛ × 12″ strip of tan synthetic suede • Acrylic paints: white, black, light apricot, dark red-brown, and medium-pink • High-gloss finish

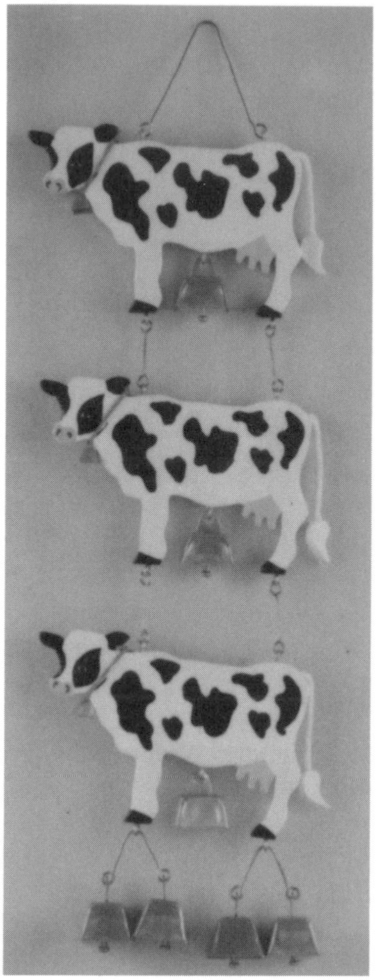

Cow Wind Chimes

Cow Wind Chimes*

1. Cut one body (20–1) from ½ × 5½ pine lattice (top cow) and two bodies (20–1) from ¼ × 5¼ pine lattice (middle and bottom cows).

2. Cut three tail tips (20–2) from ¼ × 5¼ pine lattice.

3. Using the 1⁄16″ bit, drill ¼″-deep tail holes into each cow and tail tip where indicated by the small arrows on 20–1 and 20–2.

4. Paint both sides of the cows in the same manner, extending the colors onto the edge surfaces, except where indicated. Use white to paint the bodies and tail tips. Paint the ears, spots, and hooves black. Use light apricot to paint the muzzles, extending the color slightly onto the edge surface of the chins. Paint the eyes white and the pupils black. Paint the nostrils and irises dark red-brown and the udders medium-pink.

5. Apply the high-gloss finish to each cow.

6. Cut the yarn into three 2¼″ lengths. For each cow, use tacky glue to adhere one end of the yarn into the hole in the tail tip. Making sure that the tail tip points up, adhere the opposite end of the yarn into the tail hole in the cow.

7. Use an ice pick to make ⅛″-deep pilot holes in each cow where indicated by the large arrows on 20–1.

---

*Refer to the General Directions for the techniques needed to complete this project.

8. Use the two adjustable pliers to slightly pry open three screw eyes. Hook the medium bells onto the screw eyes, and close the screw eyes with the pliers. Thread a screw eye–bell assembly into the pilot hole in the underside of each cow. Have a long side of each bell parallel with the body.

9. Thread the remaining screw eyes into the rest of the pilot holes. Make sure that the holes are at right angles to the bodies, as shown in the photograph.

10. Cut the wire to the lengths described below. Use the needle-nose pliers to form ³⁄₁₆″-diameter loops at the ends of each wire. Make sure that the openings in both loops in each wire face the same side of the wire. To attach the wires, pry the loops slightly open, hook them onto the screw eyes, and then close the loops.

  a. Cut a 6½″ length of wire for the hanger. With the loop openings facing up, bend the wire in the middle to form an inverted V. Attach the loops to the screw eyes in the upper surface of the top cow.

  b. Cut four 2⅛″ lengths of wire. With the loop openings facing outwards, hook two wires onto the screw eyes in the hooves of the top cow and then onto the screw eyes in the upper surface of the middle cow. Attach the middle cow to the bottom cow in the same manner.

  c. Cut two 1½″ lengths of wire. Insert each wire through a screw eye in the bottom cow's hoof and form loops at the ends of the wire. With the loops facing up, bend the wire in the middle to form an inverted V. Attach the large bells to the loops.

11. Cut the synthetic suede into three 4″ strips. Thread a small bell onto a suede strip for each cow. Tie the ends into a knot at the back of the cow's neck, trimming the ends close to the knot.

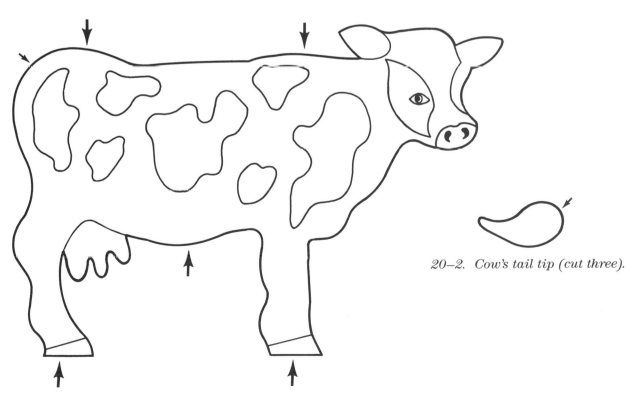

20–1. Cow's body (cut three).

20–2. Cow's tail tip (cut three).

21. Horse Weather Vane

Horse Weather Vane

MATERIALS

- 8″ length of ¼ × 5¼ clear pine lattice
- 42″ length of ½ × 5½ clear pine lattice
- 15″ length of ³⁄₁₆″ dowelling
- 5⅛″ length of ⁵⁄₁₆″ dowelling
- 7⅝″ length of ⁷⁄₁₆″ dowelling
- Drill bits: ³⁄₁₆″ and ¹⁵⁄₆₄″
- Acrylic paint: very dark red-brown
- Satin finish

Horse*

1. Cut one body (21–1), one right front leg (21–2), one left front leg (21–3), and two back legs (21–4) from ½ × 5½ pine lattice.

2. Cut one tail (21–5), one mane (21–6), one forelock (21–7), and two ears (21–8) from ¼ × 5¼ pine lattice.

3. Using the ¹⁵⁄₆₄″ bit, drill a ⁵⁄₁₆″-deep tail hole where indicated by the large arrow on the back of the body (21–1).

4. Using the ³⁄₁₆″ bit, drill a ½″-deep hole where indicated by the large arrow on the bottom of the body (21–1).

5. Round the edges of the tail's peg (21–5) by whittling so that it will fit snugly into the tail hole at the back of the body (21–1). Glue the tail peg into the tail hole.

6. Glue the mane (21–6) to the back of the head between the small arrows on 21–1.

7. Glue the forelock (21–7) to the forehead, matching the dot at its tip to the dot on 21–1.

8. Glue the ears (21–8) to the sides of the head, where indicated by the dashed line on 21–1.

9. Glue the right front (21–2) and right back (21–4) legs to the right side of the body where indicated by the heavy dashed lines on 21–1. Glue the left front (21–3) and left back (21–4) legs to the left side of the body where indicated by the light dashed lines on 21–1.

---

*Refer to the General Directions for the techniques needed to complete this project.

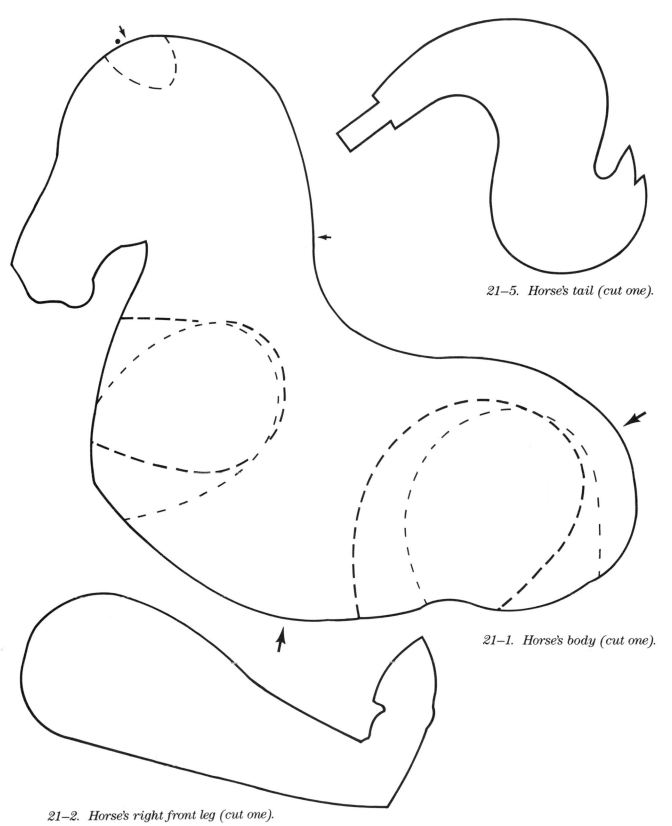

21-5. Horse's tail (cut one).

21-1. Horse's body (cut one).

21-2. Horse's right front leg (cut one).

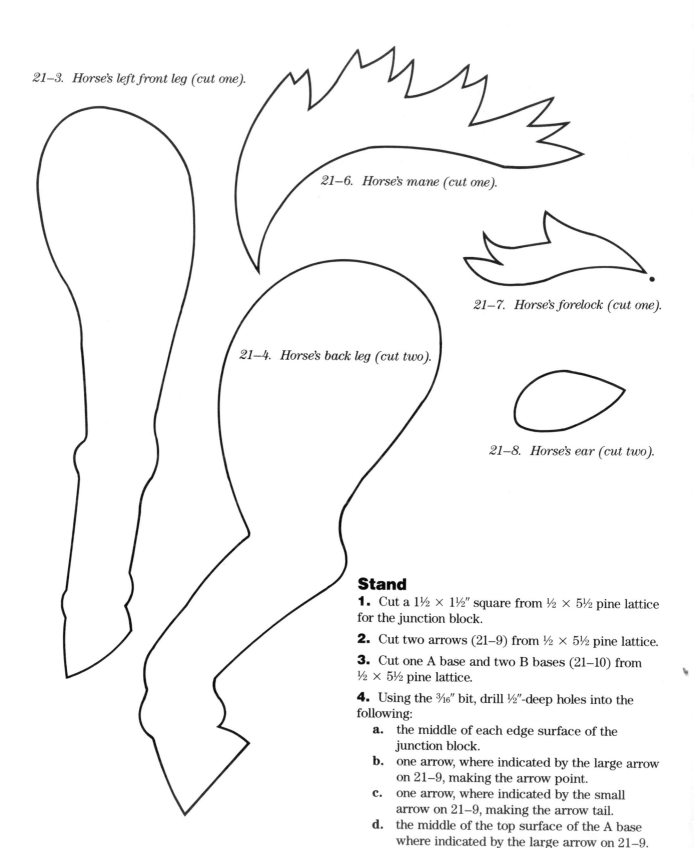

21–3. Horse's left front leg (cut one).

21–6. Horse's mane (cut one).

21–7. Horse's forelock (cut one).

21–4. Horse's back leg (cut two).

21–8. Horse's ear (cut two).

Stand

1. Cut a 1½ × 1½″ square from ½ × 5½ pine lattice for the junction block.

2. Cut two arrows (21–9) from ½ × 5½ pine lattice.

3. Cut one A base and two B bases (21–10) from ½ × 5½ pine lattice.

4. Using the ³⁄₁₆″ bit, drill ½″-deep holes into the following:

    a. the middle of each edge surface of the junction block.

    b. one arrow, where indicated by the large arrow on 21–9, making the arrow point.

    c. one arrow, where indicated by the small arrow on 21–9, making the arrow tail.

    d. the middle of the top surface of the A base where indicated by the large arrow on 21–9.

5. With the bottom edges even, glue the B bases to the centers of both sides of the A base (21–10).

6. Cut dowelling to the lengths listed in the Table.

Table: Dowelling Lengths

Part	Dowelling	Length
Upper post	$5/16''$	$5\frac{1}{8}''$
Lower post	$7/16''$	$7\frac{5}{8}''$
Front arrow shaft	$3/16''$	$7''$
Rear arrow shaft	$3/16''$	$6''$

7. Whittle $\frac{1}{2}''$ of both ends of the upper and lower posts into $\frac{3}{16}''$-diameter pegs.

8. Glue the upper post into the hole in the bottom of the horse and into one hole in the junction block. As shown in the photograph, have the face surfaces of the junction block and the horse on the same plane.

9. Glue the lower post into the bottom hole of the junction block and into the base. Angle the base, as shown in the photograph.

10. Glue the front and rear arrow shafts into the junction block, and glue the shafts into the arrow point and tail.

11. Paint the assembly very dark red-brown.

12. Apply the satin finish.

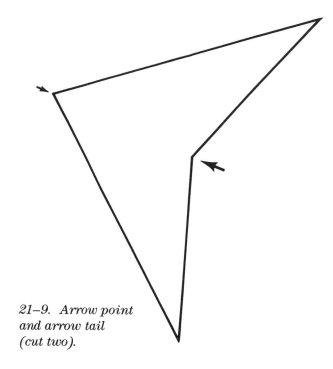

21–9. Arrow point and arrow tail (cut two).

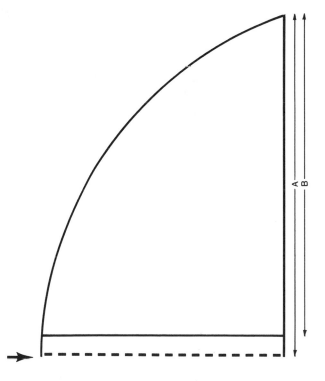

21–10. Half-pattern for the A base (cut one), and the pattern for the B base (cut two).

22. Decorative Watermelon Slices

Decorative Watermelon Slices

Decorative Watermelon Slices*

1. Cut one large (22–1) and one small (22–2) watermelon slice from 1 × 10 pine.

2. Paint both sides of each in the same manner, extending the paint colors onto the edge surfaces. Paint the flesh bright red and the outer rind medium-yellow-green.

3. Sponge dark pink paint on top of the flesh, using a 2 × 2″ sponge. Apply the paint densely at the inner-rind outline and progressively lighter towards the tip of the slice. (See the color section.)

4. Using a ½ × ½″ sponge, sponge the inner rind pale grey-green, extending the paint slightly onto both the flesh and the outer rind.

5. Paint the watermelon seeds black.

6. Apply the high-gloss finish.

---

*Refer to the General Directions for the techniques needed to complete this project.

MATERIALS

- 16″ length of 1 × 10 clear pine
- Acrylic paints: bright red, medium-yellow-green, dark pink, pale grey-green, and black
- High-gloss finish

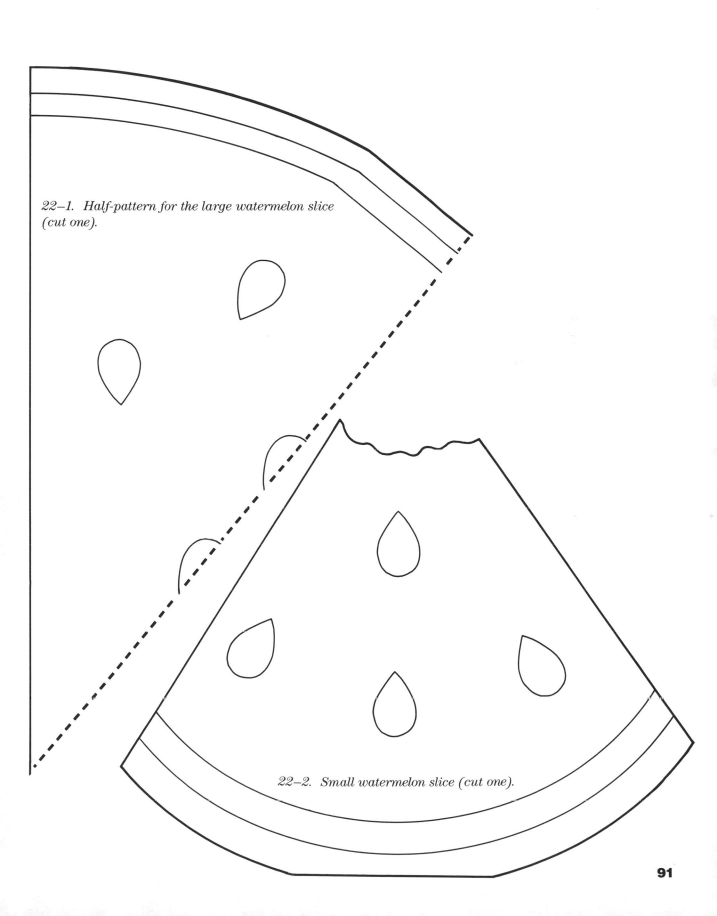

22–1. Half-pattern for the large watermelon slice (cut one).

22–2. Small watermelon slice (cut one).

91

23. Red Barn Wall Clock

Red Barn Wall Clock

Red Barn Wall Clock*

1. Cut a 1⅝ × 10¾″ rectangle from ½ × 5½ pine lattice for the base.

2. Cut one barn (23–1) from 1 × 10 pine. To cut the opening for the clock insert, drill a hole, using the ⅜″ bit, where indicated by the star on the pattern. Thread the scroll-saw blade through the hole and cut the opening. Release the saw blade to remove the barn. The outside diameter of the clock's face is indicated by the dashed circle on the pattern.

3. Cut one each of the following patterns from ¼ × 5¼ pine lattice: silo (23–2), silo roof (23–3), tree (23–4), bush (23–5), rooster (23–6), cow (23–7), cow's tail tip (23–8), and hay (23–9).

4. Transfer the outlines of the tinted (gluing) areas onto the fronts of the barn (23–1), silo (23–2), tree (23–4), and bush (23–5).

---

*Refer to the General Directions for the techniques needed to complete this project.

MATERIALS

- 35″ length of ¼ × 5¼ clear pine lattice
- 12″ length of ½ × 5½ clear pine lattice
- 10″ length of 1 × 10 clear pine
- Three white, 12-mm, regular-hole, round wood beads
- Drill bits: No. 61 (wire gauge), ⅟₁₆″, and ⅜″
- Fifteen #19 × ½″ wire brads
- Three #18 × ¾″ wire brads
- One ½″-long × ¼″-diameter screw eye
- One 2½″-long sawtooth hanger, with supplied brads
- Two adjustable pliers
- 1 × 6″ rectangle of white decorative adhesive covering
- 2⅝″ length of white worsted-weight cotton yarn
- One ¼ × ¼ × ¼″ copper bell
- 3⁵⁄₁₆″-diameter (2¼″ mounting diameter) quartz clock insert
- Acrylic paints: bright red, black, medium-olive-green, light grey, medium-red-brown, white, dark yellow, medium-pink, and light yellow
- High-gloss finish

5. Transfer the dashed lines on 23–5 and 23–7 onto the backs of the bush and cow.

6. Cut two 1⅜ × 3⁷⁄₁₆″ rectangles from ¼ × 5¼ pine lattice for the roof gable.

7. Cut two 1⅜ × 3½″ rectangles from ¼ × 5¼ pine lattice for the roof eaves. Tilt the scroll-saw table to 34 degrees, and trim one short edge of each piece to a bevel.

8. Draw a line ¼″ from and parallel with one long edge (back) of each roof gable and eave piece. On the line, mark two points ½″ from each short edge. Using the No. 61 bit, drill pilot holes through the roof pieces at each mark.

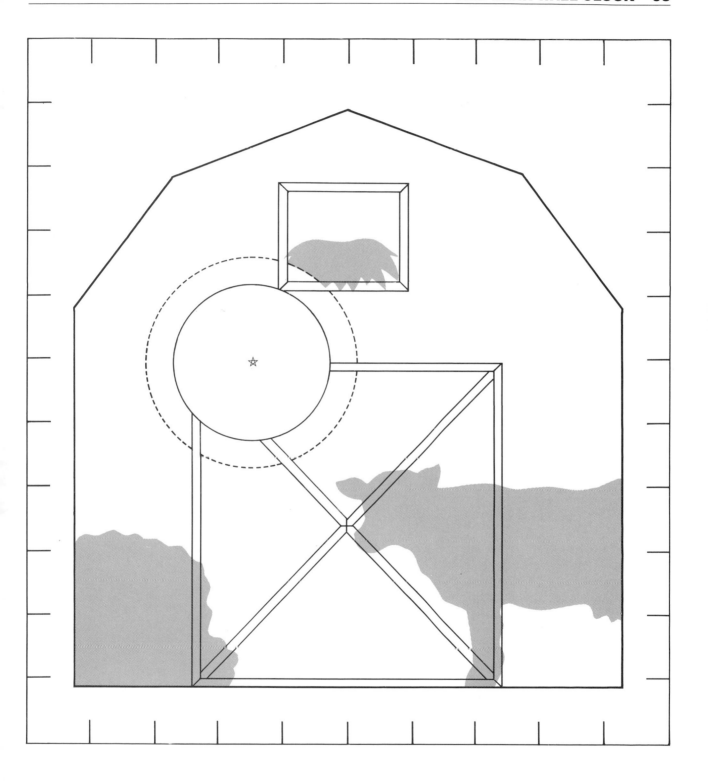

23–1. Barn. Each square equals 1". Enlarge and cut one.

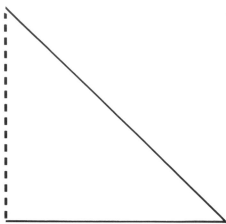

23–3. Half-pattern for the silo roof (cut one).

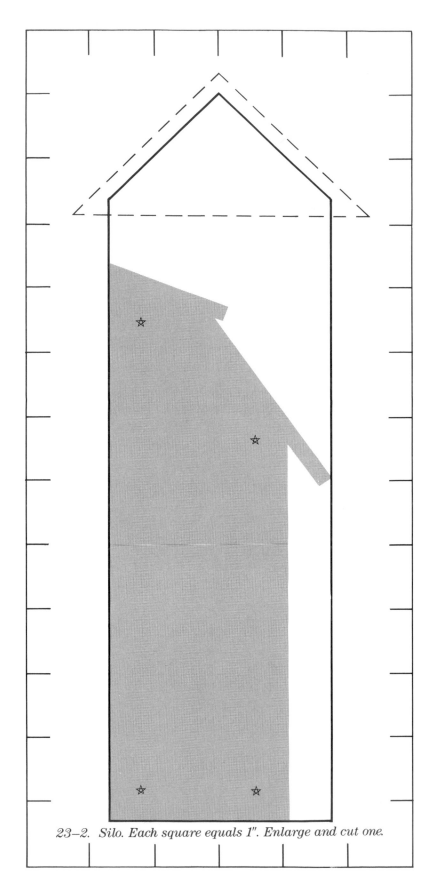

23–2. Silo. Each square equals 1". Enlarge and cut one.

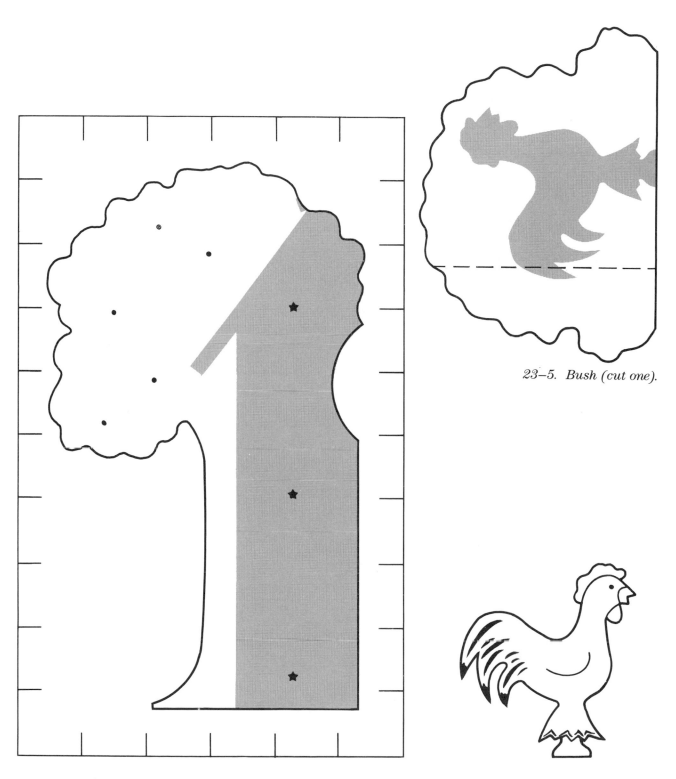

23–5. Bush (cut one).

23–4. Tree. Each square equals 1″. Enlarge and cut one.

23–6. Rooster (cut one).

9. Using the No. 61 bit, drill pilot holes through the silo (23–2) and tree (23–4), where indicated by the stars on the patterns.

10. Using the 1/16″ bit, drill 1/4″-deep holes in the cow (23–7) and the cow's tail tip (23–8), where indicated by the small arrows on the patterns.

11. Draw a line 5/8″ from and parallel with one long edge (back) of the base. Measuring from the left short edge, mark the following three points on the line: 1 5/8″, 5 3/8″, and 9 1/8″. Using the No. 61 bit, drill pilot holes through the base at each mark.

12. Glue the barn onto the base, positioning it 1 5/16″ from the left short edge and 1/4″ from the back edge of the base. Secure with three #18 × 3/4″ brads nailed through the pilot holes in the base.

13. Butt the gable pieces together at the barn's peak. Sand the butted end of each piece to a slight angle, until they fit tightly together.

14. Glue the gable pieces to the top edge of the barn. Have their back edges flush with the back of the barn. Secure with two #19 × 1/2″ brads nailed through the pilot holes in each piece.

15. Glue each eave piece under a gable piece, with its eave angle facing up. Have the back edge flush with the back of the barn. Secure with two #19 × 1/2″ brads nailed through the pilot holes in each piece.

16. Glue the silo roof (23–3) to the front of the silo (23–2), where indicated by the dashed line on 23–2.

17. Paint the individual pieces as described in a–g. Remember to paint 1/16″ into the gluing outlines and extend the colors onto the edge surfaces. Don't paint the backs of the items unless instructed.

    a. Paint the barn (23–1) bright red, the hay-loft window and the roof black, and the base medium-olive-green.

    b. Paint the silo (23–2) light grey and the silo roof (23–3) black.

    c. Paint the tree top (23–4) medium-olive green and its trunk medium-red-brown.

    d. Paint the bush (23–5) medium-olive-green. Also, paint the back portion of the bush up to the dashed line.

    e. Paint the rooster's body (23–6) white, the feet and beak dark yellow, and the wattles and

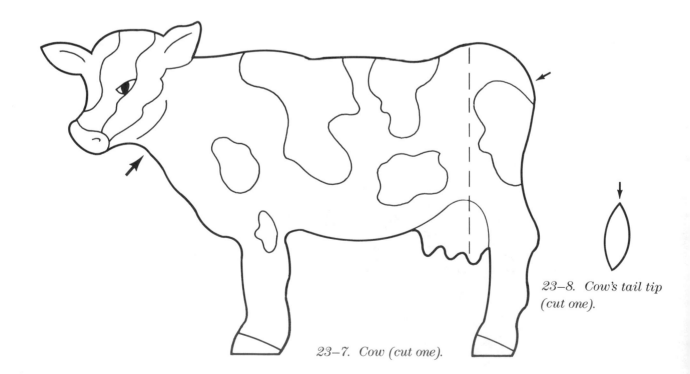

23–8. Cow's tail tip (cut one).

23–7. Cow (cut one).

comb bright red. Use black to paint the eye and the details of the wing, tailfeathers, and leg ruff.

f.   Paint the cow's body (23–7) white, including the back of the cow up to the dashed line. Use black to paint the spots, ears, nostril, eye outline and pupil, jaw outline, and hooves. Paint the ear details white. Use medium-pink to paint the muzzle and udders. Paint the tail tip (23–8) black.

g.   Paint the hay (23–9) light yellow. Paint the hay details medium-red-brown. (See the color section.)

18. Split the beads in half for the apples. (Discard one half-bead). Paint the apples bright red.

19. With the half-holes held at various angles, use tacky glue to adhere the apples to the tree top where indicated by the dots on 23–4.

20. Glue the silo assembly to the back of the barn (23–1) where indicated by the gluing outline on 23–2. Secure with four #19 × ½″ brads nailed through the pilot holes in the silo.

21. Glue the tree (23–4) to the back of the barn where indicated by the gluing outline on 23–4. Secure with three #19 × ½″ brads nailed through the pilot holes in the tree.

22. Glue the rooster (23–6) to the bush (23–5) where indicated by the gluing outline on 23–5.

23. Paint the back of the barn assembly black.

24. Apply the high-gloss finish to the painted areas only of the barn assembly, bush assembly, cow, cow's tail tip, and hay.

25. Cut six ⅛ × 6″ strips of white decorative adhesive covering for the barn door and four ⅛ × 2″ strips for the outline of the hay-loft window.

26. Adhere the strips to the barn, where indicated on 23–1, mitring all corners with a craft knife.

27. Use the 2⅝″ length of cotton yarn for the cow's tail. Use tacky glue to adhere one end of the yarn into the hole in the tail tip and the opposite end into the hole in the cow.

28. Use an ice pick to make a ⅛″-deep pilot hole in the cow for the screw eye, where indicated by the large arrow on 23–7.

29. Use the two adjustable pliers to slightly pry open the screw eye. Hook the bell onto the screw eye, and close it with the pliers. Thread the screw eye into the pilot hole in the cow.

30. Glue the cow, bush assembly, and hay to the front of the barn where indicated by the gluing outlines on 23–1.

31. Nail the sawtooth hanger to the back of the barn, centered 1″ below the roof peak. Fit the clock insert into the opening.

23–9. Hay (cut one).

24. Sweet-Pepper Napkin Holder

Sweet-Pepper Napkin Holder

Sweet-Pepper Napkin Holder*

1. Cut six peppers (24–1) from ½ × 5½ pine lattice. The pattern shows the orientation of the middle and right peppers; the left peppers are mirror images.

2. Cut six pepper calyxes (24–2) from ¼ × 5¼ pine lattice. The pattern shows the orientation of the middle and right pepper calyxes; the left pepper calyxes are mirror images.

3. Using the No. 61 bit, drill four pilot holes, where indicated by the small stars on 24–1, through two middle peppers.

4. Using the ¹⁄₁₆″ bit, drill pilot holes, where indicated by the large star on 24–1, through two right and two left peppers.

---

*Refer to the General Directions for the techniques needed to complete this project.

MATERIALS

- 6″ length of ¼ × 5¼ clear pine lattice
- 30″ length of ½ × 5½ clear pine lattice
- 5½″ length of 1 × 4 clear pine
- Four ½″-diameter oval-top screw hole plugs
- Drill bits: No. 61 (wire gauge) and ¹⁄₁₆″
- Four #6 × ¾″ flat-head wood screws
- Eight #18 × ¾″ wire brads
- Acrylic paints: bright red, dark yellow, medium-olive-green, light yellow-green, and khaki
- High-gloss finish

5. Use the 5½″ length of 1 × 4 pine for the base. Glue the flat end of each plug to each corner on the underside of the base.

6. Glue the calyxes (24–2) to the peppers (24–1) where indicated by the dashed lines on 24–1.

7. To assemble the peppers, glue a middle pepper on top of a right and left pepper, where indicated by the dashed lines on 24–1. Secure with brads nailed through the pilot holes in the middle pepper.

8. Center each pepper assembly on a long-side edge of the base. Have the bottoms of the left and right peppers extend ⅟₁₆″ below the bottom edge of the base. On the backs of the left and right peppers, outline the position of the base.

9. Paint one pepper assembly as follows: left pepper medium-olive-green, middle pepper dark red, and right pepper dark yellow. Paint the other pepper assembly as follows: left pepper dark red, middle pepper dark yellow, and right pepper medium-olive-green. (Don't paint into the outlined areas on the backs of the pepper assemblies or into the pilot holes.) Paint the calyxes and stems medium-olive-green. Repeat the calyx pattern on the backs of the dark yellow peppers and paint a curve for the base of each dark red pepper's stem. (See the color section.)

10. Using a 1 × 1″ sponge, sponge light yellow-green highlights in a ¼″-wide band on the bottoms of the calyxes and the sides of the stems.

11. Omitting both long-side edges, paint the base khaki.

12. Glue the pepper assemblies to the long-side edges of the base, and secure with screws driven through the pilot holes in the right and left peppers.

13. Finish painting the base.

14. Apply the high gloss finish.

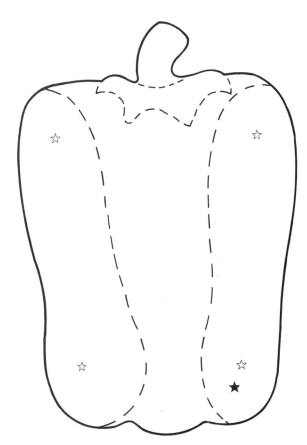

24–1. Pepper (cut six).

24–2. Pepper calyx (cut six).

25. Eggplant Paper-Towel Dispenser

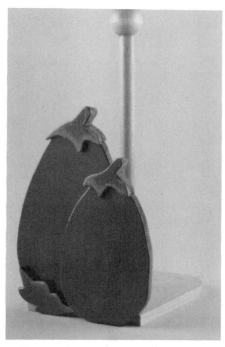

Eggplant Paper-Towel Dispenser

MATERIALS

- 6″ length of ¼ × 5¼ clear pine lattice
- 27″ length of ½ × 5½ clear pine lattice
- 2″ length of ⁵⁄₁₆″ dowelling (or a diameter that fits snugly into the hole of the 35.5-mm bead)
- 11⅛″ length of ¾″ dowelling
- One 35.5-mm, unfinished, round wood bead
- Drill bits: No. 61 (wire gauge), ¹⁄₁₆″, and ⁵⁄₁₆″ (Note: Use a bit that matches the diameter of the 2″ length of dowelling.)
- One #8 × 1¾″ flat-head wood screw
- Four #16 × 1¼″ wire brads
- Two #18 × ¾″ wire brads
- Acrylic paints: dark purple, medium-olive-green, and light yellow-green
- High-gloss finish

Eggplant Paper-Towel Dispenser*

1. Cut one base (25–1), one large eggplant (25–2), and one small eggplant (25–3) from ½ × 5½ pine lattice. Transfer the outline of the tinted (gluing) area onto the large eggplant (25–2).

2. Cut one large stem (25–4), one small stem (25–5), and one leaf (25–6) from ¼ × 5¼ pine lattice.

3. Using the ¹⁄₁₆″ bit, drill a pilot hole for the ¾″ dowelling through the base where indicated by the large star on 25–1.

---

*Refer to the General Directions for the techniques needed to complete this project.

4. Using the No. 61 bit, drill pilot holes only through the left side of the base where indicated by the small stars on 25–1.

5. Using the No. 61 bit, drill pilot holes through the small eggplant (25–3) and the leaf (25–6) where indicated by the stars on the patterns.

6. Using the ¹⁄₁₆″ bit, drill a ¼″-deep pilot hole into the middle of one end of the ¾″ dowelling (bottom). Use a ⁵⁄₁₆″ bit to drill a ⁷⁄₁₆″-deep hole into the middle of the other end (top). (See the note in the Materials list.)

7. Glue one end of the 2″ length of ⁵⁄₁₆″ dowelling into the top hole in the ¾″ dowelling and the other end into the hole in the 35.5-mm bead. Sand off the dowelling edges that extend from the top of the bead.

8. Glue the large and small stems (25–4 and 25–5) to the tops of the large and small eggplants (25–2

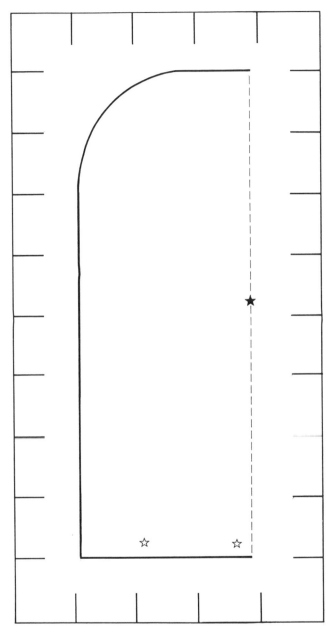

25–1. Half-pattern for the dispenser's base. Each square equals 1″. Enlarge and cut one.

and 25–3) where indicated by the dashed lines on the patterns.

9. Position the large eggplant (25–2) on the base (25–1) and flush with its front edge. Align the dots on 25–2 with the pilot holes in the base. Glue the bottom of the eggplant to the base, and secure with two #16 × 1¼″ brads nailed from the underside of the base.

10. Glue the small eggplant (25–3) to the large eggplant, where indicated by the dashed line on 25–2. Nail the bottom edge of the small eggplant to the front edge of the base, using two #16 × 1¼″ brads nailed through the pilot holes in the small eggplant.

11. Paint the eggplants dark purple. Paint ¹⁄₁₆″ into the gluing outline on the large eggplant (25–2).

12. Paint the stems medium-olive-green, both front and back. Paint the leaf medium-olive-green, extending the paint onto the edge surfaces and ¹⁄₁₆″ onto the back.

13. Using a 1 × 1″ sponge, sponge light yellow-green highlights in a ¼″-wide band around the stems. (Don't sponge the right side of the stem tips.) Referring to the photograph, use light yellow-green to sponge a highlight onto the top left and right sides of the leaf.

14. Glue the leaf to both the front of the large eggplant and the front edge of the base. Secure with two #18 × ¾″ brads nailed through the pilot holes in the leaf.

15. Apply glue to the bottom end of the ¾″ dowelling, and secure it to the base by driving the screw into the dowelling from the underside of the base.

16. Apply the high-gloss finish.

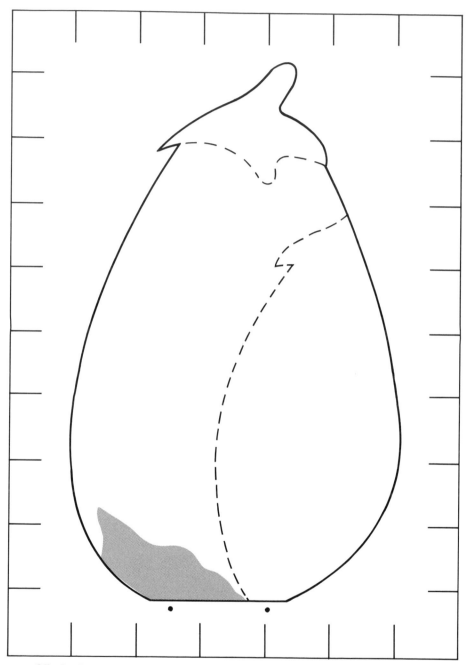

25–2. Large eggplant. Each square equals 1". Enlarge and cut one.

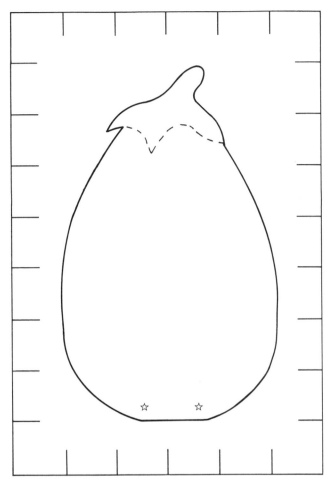

*25–3. Small eggplant. Each square equals 1".
Enlarge and cut one.*

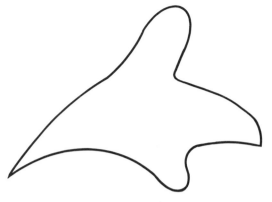

25–4. Large eggplant's stem (cut one).

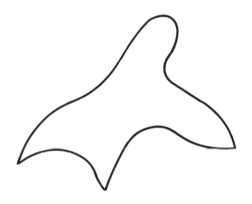

25–5. Small eggplant's stem (cut one).

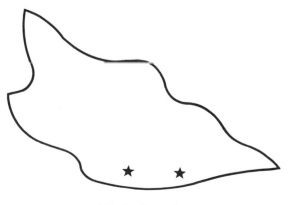

25–6. Leaf (cut one).

26. Carrot-Bunch Utensil Rack

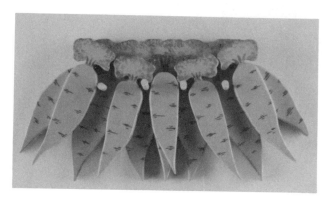

Carrot-Bunch Utensil Rack

MATERIALS

- 26″ length of ½ × 5½ clear pine lattice
- 12″ length of ¼″ dowelling
- Drill bits: No. 61 (wire gauge) and ¼″
- Ten #18 × ¾″ wire brads
- Two 1½″-long sawtooth hangers, with supplied brads
- Acrylic paints: medium-orange, light yellow-green, dark green, and black
- Satin finish

Carrot-Bunch Utensil Rack*

1. Cut five carrots (26–1) and one base (26–2) from ½ × 5½ pine lattice. For the middle carrot, cut the top off one carrot, where indicated by the dashed line on 26–1. The carrot pattern (26–1) shows the orientation of the middle and two right carrots; the two left carrots are mirror images.

2. Transfer the outlines of the tinted (gluing) areas on 26–2 onto the base. Position the middle carrot on the middle front of the base, with its top edge 1⁵⁄₁₆″ from the top edge of the base. Trace the outline of the middle carrot onto the base.

3. Cut four 2¼″ lengths of dowelling for the pegs.

4. Using the No. 61 bit, drill pilot holes through the base where indicated by the dots on 26–2.

5. Using the ¼″ bit, drill four ¼″-deep peg holes into the front of the base where indicated by the stars on 26–2.

6. Paint the base, using medium-orange for the carrots and light yellow-green for the carrot tops. Paint ¹⁄₁₆″ into the gluing outlines, and don't paint into the peg holes. Extend all colors onto the edge

---

*Refer to the General Directions for the techniques needed to complete this project.

26–1. Carrot (cut five).

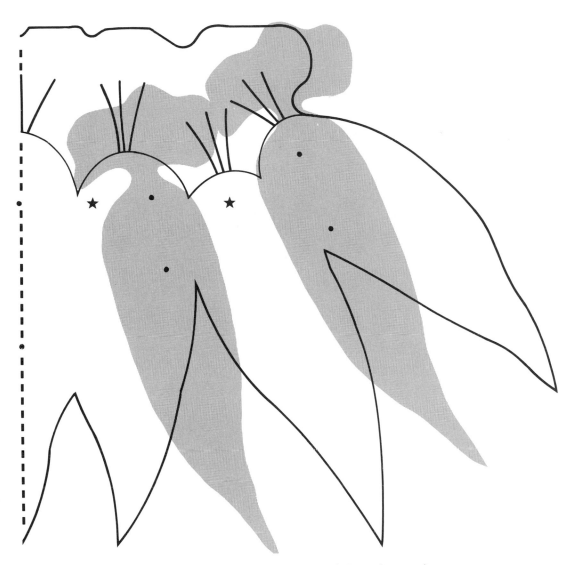

26–2. Half-pattern for the rack's base (cut one).

surfaces. As shown in the photograph, sponge a dark green border onto the carrot tops, using a 1 × 1″ sponge. Use dark green to paint the carrot-top stems. Use black to paint the carrot details, shown in the photograph.

7. Paint the five carrots in the same manner. (Don't paint the backs of the carrots at this point.)

8. Glue the carrots to the base, and secure with ten brads nailed into the pilot holes from the back of the base.

9. Now continue the paint colors onto the back of the assembly.

10. Glue the pegs into the peg holes.

11. Apply the satin finish.

12. Nail the sawtooth hangers to the back of the base, spacing them ½″ from the top edge and sides.

27. Watermelon Place Mat

Watermelon Place Mat

Watermelon Place Mat*

1. Cut one watermelon (27–1) from ¼″ plywood.

2. Paint both sides in the same manner, extending the paint colors onto the edge surfaces. Paint the flesh bright red and the outer rind medium-yellow-green.

3. Sponge dark pink paint on top of the flesh, using a 2 × 2″ sponge. Apply the paint densely at the inner-rind outline and progressively lighter towards the middle. (See the color section.)

4. Using a ½ × ½″ sponge, sponge the inner rind pale grey-green, extending the paint slightly onto both the flesh and the outer rind.

5. Paint the watermelon seeds black.

6. Apply the high-gloss waterproof finish.

MATERIALS

- 14 × 22″ rectangle of ¼″ birch plywood
- Acrylic paints: bright red, medium-yellow-green, dark pink, pale grey-green, and black
- High-gloss waterproof finish

---

*Refer to the General Directions for the techniques needed to complete this project. Materials and directions are for one place mat.

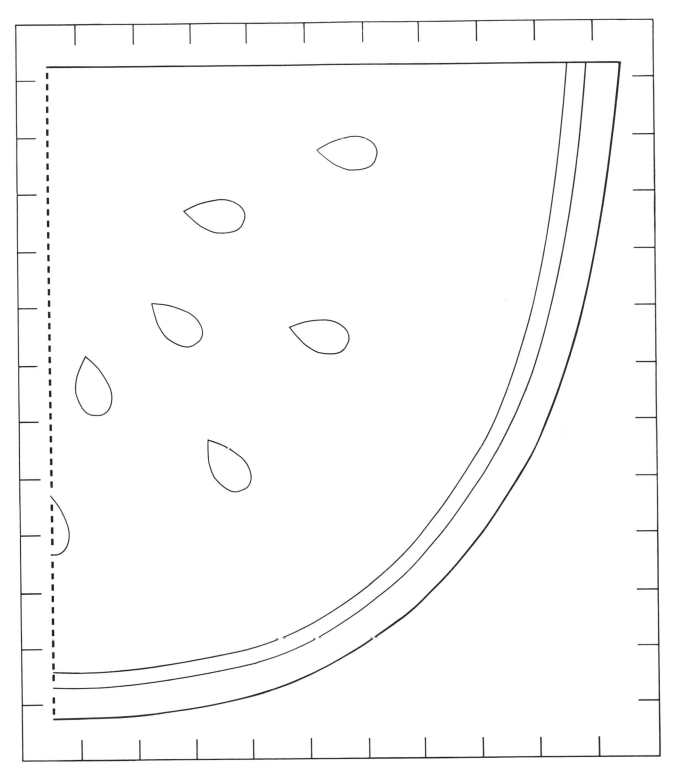

27–1. Half-pattern for the watermelon. Each square equals 1". Enlarge and cut one.

28. Strawberry Napkin Ring

Strawberry Napkin Ring

Strawberry Napkin Ring*

1. Cut one strawberry (28–1) from ½ × 5½ pine lattice.

2. Cut one calyx (28–2) from ¼ × 5¼ pine lattice.

3. Using the ⁵⁄₃₂″ bit, drill a ¼″-deep peg hole into the middle-top surface of the strawberry, where indicated by the arrow on 28–1. (The shank of the axle peg, used for the stem, will extend ⅜″ above the calyx [28–2] after assembly.)

4. Using the ⁵⁄₃₂″ bit, drill a peg hole through the calyx where indicated by the star on 28–2.

5. Paint both sides of the strawberry in the same manner. (Don't paint into the peg hole.) Paint the strawberry dark pink and the seeds black, continuing the seeds onto the outside-edge surface.

MATERIALS

- 4″ length of ¼ × 5¼ clear pine lattice
- 5½″ length of ½ × 5½ clear pine lattice
- One ⅞″-long × ⁵⁄₃₂″-diameter wooden axle peg
- Drill bit: ⁵⁄₃₂″
- Acrylic paints: dark pink, black, and medium-olive-green
- High-gloss finish

---

*Refer to the General Directions for the techniques needed to complete this project. Materials and directions are for one napkin ring.

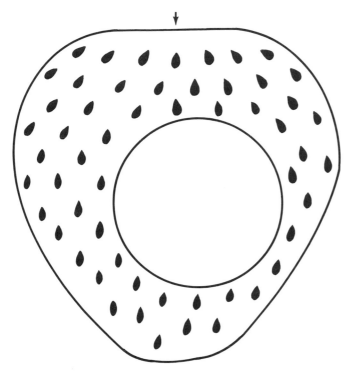

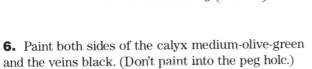

28–1. Strawberry (cut one).

28–2. Strawberry calyx (cut one).

6. Paint both sides of the calyx medium-olive-green and the veins black. (Don't paint into the peg hole.)

7. Apply a small amount of glue into the calyx and strawberry peg holes. Insert the axle peg through the peg hole in the calyx and then into the peg hole

in the strawberry.

8. Use medium-olive-green to paint the portion of the axle peg that extends above the calyx.

9. Apply the high-gloss finish.

29. Wheelbarrow Condiment Holder

Wheelbarrow Condiment Holder

Wheelbarrow Condiment Holder*

1. Cut two sides (29–1), two handles (29–2), and two wheel supports (29–3) from ¼ × 5¼ pine lattice.

2. Cut one front and one back (29–4) from ½ × 5½ pine lattice.

3. Cut a 4⅛" length of 1 × 1 pine for the handle brace and a ⅞" length for the wheel-support brace.

4. Trim the shank of each axle peg to ¹¹⁄₁₆".

5. Using the No. 61 bit, drill pilot holes through the sides (29–1) and the front and back (29–4) where indicated by the stars on the patterns.

---

*Refer to the General Directions for the techniques needed to complete this project.

MATERIALS

- 48" length of ¼ × ⅞ clear pine lattice
- 38" length of ¼ × 5¼ clear pine lattice
- 14" length of ½ × 5½ clear pine lattice
- 6" length of 1 × 1 clear pine
- Two 1⁷⁄₁₆"-long × ⅜"-diameter wooden axle pegs
- One 2¼"-diameter wooden wheel (⅜" axle hole)
- Drill bits: No. 61 (wire gauge) and ⅜"
- Twelve #19 × ½" wire brads
- Eighteen #18 × ¾" wire brads
- Two ⅜" flat washers
- Acrylic paint: medium-grey-blue, white, and bright red
- High-gloss finish

29–1. Half-pattern for the wheelbarrow's sides (cut two).

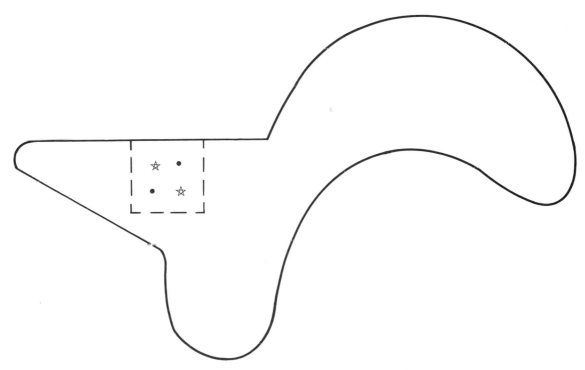

29–2. Wheelbarrow's handle (cut two).

6. Using the No. 61 bit, drill pilot holes through one handle (29–2), where indicated by the stars on the pattern. Drill pilot holes through the other handle (29–2) where indicated by the dots on the pattern.

7. Using the No. 61 bit, drill pilot holes through one wheel support (29–3) where indicated by the small stars on the pattern. Drill pilot holes through the other wheel support (29–3) where indicated by the dots on the pattern.

8. Using the ⅜" bit, drill axle-peg holes through the wheel supports where indicated by the large star on 29–3.

9. Glue and secure the sides (29–1) to the edges of the front and back (29–2), using eight #18 × ¾" brads nailed through the pilot holes in the sides.

10. On the bottom of the assembly, measure from one corner to a corner that is diagonally opposite. Then measure the other two diagonally opposite corners. If the measurements are identical, the assembly is square. If they are not identical, gently flex the assembly until the measurements match. On

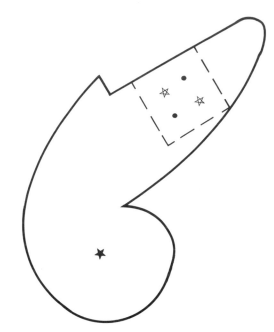

29–3. Wheelbarrow's wheel support (cut two).

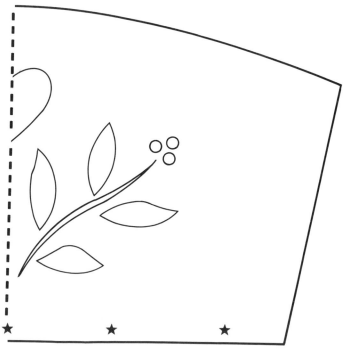

29–4. Half-pattern for the front and back of the wheelbarrow (cut two).

the bottom of the assembly, measure between the front and back for the length of the bottom slats (approximately 9¼″). Cut five slats from ¼ × ⅞ pine lattice.

11. Center the end of each slat over corresponding pilot holes in the front and back. Glue and secure, using ten #18 × ¾″ brads nailed through the front and the back.

12. On the bottom of the assembly, draw a line across the slats 1″ from and parallel with the outside back of the assembly. On the line, mark the center of each of the middle-three slats.

13. On the bottom of the assembly, draw a line across the middle slat ⅝″ from the outside front of the assembly. On the line, mark the center of the middle slat.

14. Using the No. 61 bit, drill pilot holes through the slats at each mark.

15. Glue the handle brace between the handles, where indicated by the dashed lines on 29–2. Secure with four #19 × ½″ brads nailed through the pilot holes in the handles.

16. Glue the wheel-support brace between the wheel supports where indicated by the dashed lines

on 29–3. Secure with four #19 × ½″ brads nailed through the wheel supports.

17. Glue the handle assembly to the bottom back of the wheelbarrow, centering the handle brace over the pilot holes in the slats. Secure with three #19 × ½″ brads nailed through the slats.

18. Glue the wheel-support assembly to the bottom front of the wheelbarrow, centering the wheel-support brace over the pilot hole in the middle slat. Secure with one #19 × ½″ brad nailed through the slats.

19. Paint the wheelbarrow medium-grey-blue. (Don't paint into the axle-peg holes in the wheel supports.) Use white to paint the hearts and flowers. Paint the axle-peg caps and the wheel bright red.

20. Apply the high-gloss finish to the wheelbarrow, axle-peg caps, and wheel.

21. Apply a small amount of glue to the cut end of each axle peg and a ¼″ band of glue to the shank next to each cap. Position the wheel, with a washer at each side, between the wheel supports. Insert the axle pegs through the axle-peg holes in the wheel support. The wheel should spin freely.

30. Pumpkin-Leaf Trivet

Pumpkin-Leaf Trivet

MATERIALS

- 13 × 15″ rectangle of ¼″ birch plywood
- Ten ½″-diameter oval-top screw hole plugs
- Waterproof wood glue
- Acrylic paints: medium-yellow-green and light grey-green
- High-gloss waterproof finish

Pumpkin-Leaf Trivet*

1. Cut one pumpkin leaf (30–1) from ¼″ plywood.

2. Glue the flat end of each plug to the underside of the leaf, where indicated by the dots in the drawing.

3. Paint the assembly medium-yellow-green.

4. Using a 2 × 2″ sponge, sponge light grey-green paint in a ½″- to 1″-wide, irregular border on the top surface of the trivet. (See the color section.)

5. Apply the high-gloss waterproof finish.

---

*Refer to the General Directions for the techniques needed to complete this project.

30–1. Pumpkin leaf. Each square equals 1". Enlarge and cut one.

31. Hen Measuring Spoon and Cup Rack

Hen Measuring Spoon and Cup Rack

Hen Measuring Spoon and Cup Rack*

1. Cut one body (31–1) from ½″ plywood.

2. Cut one each of the following patterns from ¼ × 5¼ pine lattice: head (31–2), wing (31–3), tail feathers (31–4), left egg (31–5), and right egg (31–6).

3. Transfer the outlines of the tinted (gluing) areas onto the fronts of the body (31–1) and the left egg (31–5). Transfer the dashed lines on 31–2 and 31–3 onto the backs of the head and wing.

Refer to the General Directions for the techniques needed to complete this project.

MATERIALS

- 14 × 14″ square of ½″ birch plywood
- 42″ length of ¼ × ⅞ clear pine lattice
- 20″ length of ¼ × 5¼ clear pine lattice
- 13″ length of ⅜″ dowelling
- 6″ length of ⁷⁄₁₆″ dowelling
- Drill bits: No. 61 (wire gauge) and ⅜″
- Fourteen #19 × ½″ wire brads
- Two 2½″-long sawtooth hangers, with supplied brads
- 2½ yards of natural-color plastic raffia
- Acrylic paints: black, bright red, dark yellow, khaki, and white
- High-gloss finish

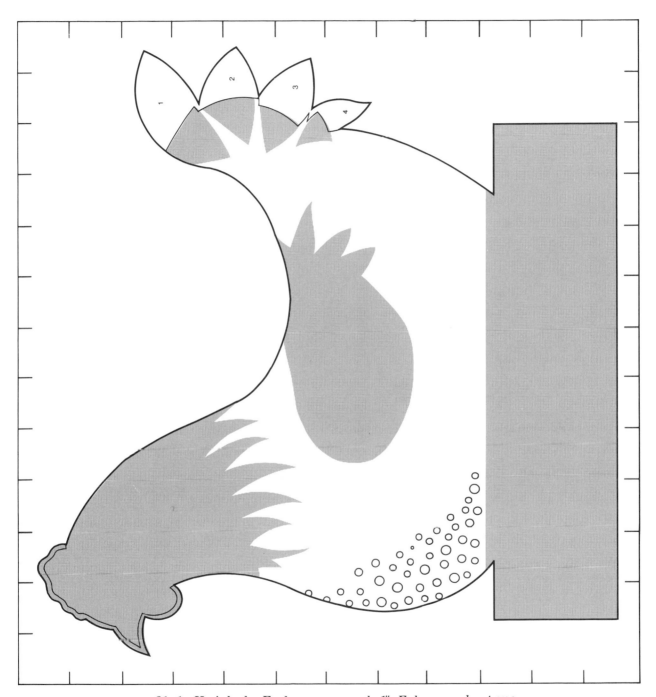

31–1. Hen's body. Each square equals 1". Enlarge and cut one.

4. Cut three 13″ lengths of ¼ × ⅞ pine lattice for the crate slats. Sand the corners to slightly round them.

5. Cut six ⅛″ lengths of ⁷⁄₁₆″ dowelling for the decorative peg caps on the crate.

6. Cut five 1¾″ lengths of ⅜″ dowelling for the hanging pegs. Soften the edge of one end of each peg by sanding.

7. Using the No. 61 bit, drill pilot holes through the head (31–2) and wing (31–3) where indicated by the stars on the patterns.

8. Using the No. 61 bit, drill pilot holes through each tail feather where indicated by the stars on 31–4.

9. Draw a line down the middle of the length of each crate slat. On the line, mark a point 2″ from each end. Using the No. 61 bit, drill pilot holes through the slats at each mark.

31–2. Hen's head (cut one).

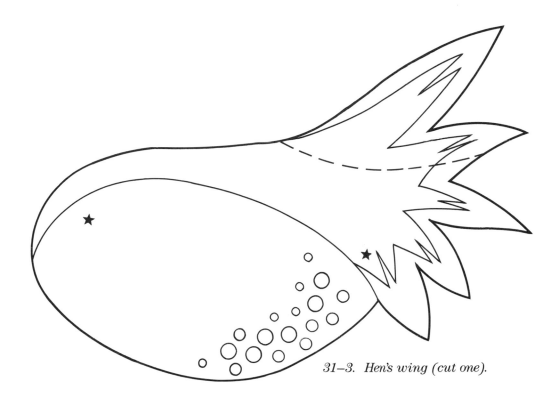

31–3. Hen's wing (cut one).

10. On the central line of one crate slat (top slat), mark 4⅜″ and 6⅝″ from the left short edge. On the central line of another crate slat (middle slat), mark 2¼″, 6½″, and 10¾″ from the left short edge. Using the ⅜″ bit, drill peg holes through the slats at each mark.

11. To create the angle on the underside of each tail feather (31–4), whittle a flat surface from the dashed line to the dot so that the thickness at the dot is ¹⁄₁₆″.

12. Glue the left egg (31–5) on top of the right egg (31–6), where indicated by the dashed line on 31–6.

13. Paint the different items as described in a–e. Remember to paint ¹⁄₁₆″ into the gluing outlines and extend the colors onto the edge surfaces, unless otherwise instructed. Don't paint the backs of the items, unless instructed.

    a. Use black to paint the bottom portion of the body and the base (31–1). Paint the tail feathers and chest spots khaki. Use white to paint the edge surfaces of the front of the neck and the back of the head. Extend the color slightly onto the front surface. Using red for the comb and wattle, and yellow for the beak, paint the edge surfaces and slightly onto the front surface, as shown by the outlines on the pattern.

    b. Paint the head (31–2) white, the comb and wattles bright red, the beak dark yellow, and the feather details khaki. Paint the back of the head up to the dashed lines. Use black to paint the nostril, eye outlines, and pupil. Paint the areas at the sides of the pupil khaki. Use white to highlight the eye at 9 o'clock.

    c. Paint the bottom of the wing (31–3) black and the top white. Use khaki to paint the feather details and spots. Paint the back of the wing up to the dashed line.

    d. Paint the tail feathers (31–4) white and the feather details khaki. Omitting the whittled area, paint the back of each tail feather khaki.

    e. Paint the egg assembly white. (Don't paint the edge surfaces of the horizontal and vertical straight edges.)

14. Glue the head (31–2) and wing (31–3) to the body where indicated by the outlines of the gluing

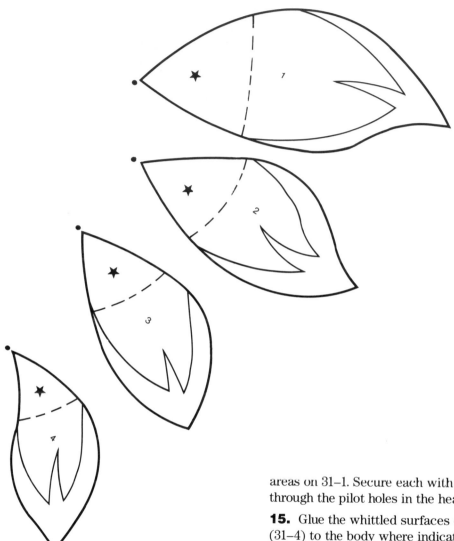

31–4. Hen's tail feathers (cut one of each).

areas on 31–1. Secure each with two brads nailed through the pilot holes in the head and wing.

15. Glue the whittled surfaces of the tail feathers (31–4) to the body where indicated by the outlines of the gluing areas on 31–1. The numbers on the tail feathers (31–4) correspond to the numbers on the body pattern (31–1). Secure with one brad nailed through the pilot hole in each tail feather.

16. Glue the crate slats to the base of the body, centering them on the width of the base. Have the bottom slat extend ⅛″ below the base, and space the slats ¹⁄₁₆″ apart. Secure each with two brads nailed through the pilot holes in the slats.

17. Glue a decorative peg cap ⅜″ from the end of each crate slat and centered on the height of the slat.

18. Glue the unsanded ends of the hanging pegs into the peg holes.

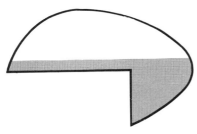

31–5. Left egg (cut one).

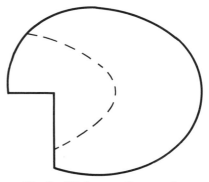

31–6. Right egg (cut one).

19. Glue the egg assembly to the back of the right side of the crate and, at the same time, to the edge surfaces of the body's base.

20. Paint the back of the assembly black.

21. Apply the high-gloss finish.

22. Cut twenty-eight 3″ lengths of raffia for the hay. Use tacky glue to adhere the ends of twelve lengths to the back of the left side of the crate. Adhere twelve lengths to the back of the egg assembly at the right. Adhere four lengths to the back of the right side of the crate, in front of the right egg. Allow the glue to dry; then tear the raffia, from tip to base, to make multiple strands.

23. Nail the sawtooth hangers to the back of the body. Position them 6″ from and parallel with the bottom of the crate and spaced ½″ from the sides of the body.

32. Apple-Harvest Refrigerator Magnets

Apple-Harvest Refrigerator Magnets

Apple-Harvest Refrigerator Magnets*

1. Cut one each of the following patterns from ¼ × 5¼ pine lattice: apple tree (32–1), apple basket (32–2), apple half (32–3), apple-pie crust (32–5), and apple-pie bottom (32–6).

2. To paint the individual pieces, refer to the Materials list for the paint color codes. Extend all colors onto the edge surfaces, and paint the back

---

*Refer to the General Directions section for the techniques needed to complete this project.

MATERIALS

- 15″ length of ¼ × 5¼ clear pine lattice
- Nineteen white, 10-mm, regular-hole, round wood beads
- Drill bit: 5⁄64″
- Scrap of medium-green synthetic suede
- Seven ¾″-diameter × 3⁄16″-thick disc magnets
- Acrylic paints: black (B), medium-yellow-green (MYG), light red-brown (LRB), dark red-brown (DRB), bright red (BR), ochre (O), and ecru (E)
- Acrylic metallic paint: silver (SM)
- High-gloss finish

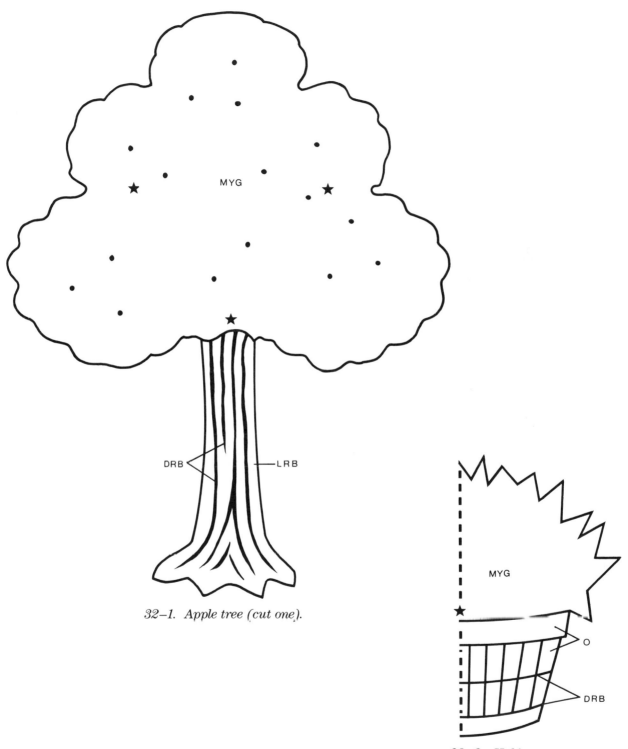

MYG

DRB ——— LRB

32–1. Apple tree (cut one).

MYG

O

DRB

*32–2. Half-pattern
for the apple basket (cut one).*

surface of each piece black. For additional painting directions, see the instructions for each piece.

3. After painting and assembling, apply the high-gloss finish.

4. Use tacky glue to adhere magnets to the back of each piece where indicated by the stars on the patterns.

5. See the instructions for the individual pieces for any additional directions.

Apple Tree

1. Split eight beads in half for the apples.

2. Paint the apples bright red. Use tacky glue to adhere the apples to the tree top where indicated by the dots on 32–1.

Apple Basket

1. Split eleven beads in half for the apples. (Discard one half-bead.)

2. Paint the apples bright red. Use tacky glue to adhere the apples to the apple leaves, as shown in the photograph.

Apple Half

1. Cut one apple leaf (32–4) from synthetic suede.

2. Using the ⁵⁄₆₄″ bit, drill a ¼″-deep leaf hole into the edge surface, where indicated by the arrow on 32–3.

3. Use black to paint the central line, the outlines of the ecru areas, and the bottom detail.

4. After applying the high-gloss finish, use tacky glue to adhere the leaf stem (32–4) into the leaf hole.

Apple Pie

1. Use dark red-brown to paint the cutouts, crimping details, and edge surface of the pie crust (32–5).

2. With the top edges even, use tacky glue to adhere the pie crust to the pie bottom (32–6).

32–3. Apple half (cut one).

32–4. Apple leaf (cut one).

32–5.   Apple-pie crust (cut one).

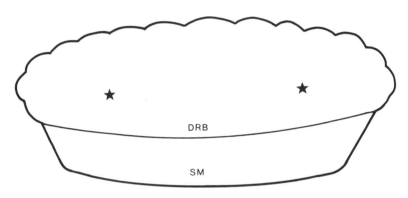

32–6.   Apple-pie bottom (cut one).

Metric Equivalents

• • • • • • • • • • • • •

Inches	MM	CM	Inches	CM	Inches	CM
⅛	3	0.3	9	22.9	30	76.2
¼	6	0.6	10	25.4	31	78.7
⅜	10	1.0	11	27.9	32	81.3
½	13	1.3	12	30.5	33	83.8
⅝	16	1.6	13	33.0	34	86.4
¾	19	1.9	14	35.6	35	88.9
⅞	22	2.2	15	38.1	36	91.4
1	25	2.5	16	40.6	37	94.0
1¼	32	3.2	17	43.2	38	96.5
1½	38	3.8	18	45.7	39	99.1
1¾	44	4.4	19	48.3	40	101.6
2	51	5.1	20	50.8	41	104.1
2½	64	6.4	21	53.3	42	106.7
3	76	7.6	22	55.9	43	109.2
3½	89	8.9	23	58.4	44	111.8
4	102	10.2	24	61.0	45	114.3
4½	114	11.4	25	63.5	46	116.8
5	127	12.7	26	66.0	47	119.4
6	152	15.2	27	68.6	48	121.9
7	178	17.8	28	71.1	49	124.5
8	203	20.3	29	73.7	50	127.0

MM—millimetres   CM—centimetres

Index